HOLY HATRED

"Fundamentalism is spreading in many parts of the world. . . . I have a dream of a world . . . where fundamentalist insanity would be unknown."

> —author Dr. Taslima Nasrin, from a speech in
> Stockholm, Sweden, August 18, 1994,
> at which she accepted a prize for her writing.
> Dr. Nasrin fled Bangladesh after clerics offered
> a $5,000 bounty for her murder.

HOLY HATRED

RELIGIOUS CONFLICTS OF THE '90s

JAMES A. HAUGHT

 Prometheus Books

59 John Glenn Drive
Amherst, New York 14228-2197

Published 1995 by Prometheus Books

99 98 97 96 95   5 4 3 2 1

Library of Congress Cataloging-in-Publication Data

Haught, James A.
    Holy hatred : religious conflicts of the '90s / James A. Haught.
            p.   cm.
    Includes bibliographical references.
    ISBN 0-87975-922-4 (alk. paper)
    1. Social conflict—Religious aspects—History—20th century. 2. Interpersonal conflict—Religious aspects—History—20th century. 3. War—Religious aspects—History—20th century. 4. World politics—1989-. 5. Religion—Controversial literature. I. Title.
BL65.S62H38   1994
305.6'09'049—dc20   94-33868
                                                          CIP

Printed in the United States of America on acid-free paper.

For Nancy, Joel, Jake, Jebb, and Cass

Contents

1

Introduction:
The New World Disorder

In Koritnik, Bosnia, in 1992, Orthodox Christian Serb gunmen herded Muslim families into a basement and tossed in grenades, then joked that the screams sounded "just like a mosque."

*　　*　　*

In Greysteel, Northern Ireland, at Halloween 1993, Protestant terrorists burst into a Catholic pub, shouted "trick or treat," and opened fire, killing seven and wounding eleven.

*　　*　　*

In India in 1992, about 2,000 Hindus and Muslims killed each other in rioting over a site where Hindus say Lord Rama was born 900,000 years ago. Meanwhile, massacres occurred in the province of Kashmir because fanatics barricaded themselves in a mosque to protect its sacred relic—a hair from Muhammad's beard.

*   *   *

In Oregon in 1993, a fundamentalist woman who shot an abortion clinic doctor called it "the most holy, the most righteous thing I've ever done." A Florida man who killed a clinic doctor was called "a hero" by a fundamentalist magazine.

*   *   *

In Saudi Arabia in 1992, an outspoken man was beheaded in public with a ceremonial sword after a religious court ruled that he had "insulted God, the holy Koran, and Muhammad the Prophet."

*   *   *

In northern Somalia in 1993, religious leaders sentenced five women to be stoned to death for adultery. Worshipers killed the women after evening prayers. Cheering onlookers videotaped the execution. United Nations observers who tried to save the women were driven off.

In Texas in 1993, besieged cultists known as the "Waco wackos" died in a fire that stunned the world.

*   *   *

In Nigeria in 1991, government officials granted permission for a German evangelist to proselytize. Muslims rioted and burned Christian churches. Christians rioted and burned Muslim mosques. Hundreds were killed.

*   *   *

In Sri Lanka in 1990, in the civil war between Buddhist Sinhalese and Hindu Tamils, Hindu gunmen entered two mosques and killed 150 Muslim worshipers because they suspected Muslims of supporting the Buddhists. In 1993, a Hindu suicide bomber killed the Buddhist president.

*   *   *

In Israel's occupied West Bank in 1994, an intensely religious Jewish doctor smuggled a machine gun into a historic mosque and murdered thirty Muslims as they knelt in prayer. The massacre triggered yet another wave of killing between Jews and Muslims.

A great irony of the 1990s is that religion—supposedly a source of kindness and human concern—has taken the lead as the foremost contributing factor to hatred, war, and terrorism. With Soviet Communism gone and the Cold War no longer spurring conflicts, the world spotlight has shifted to local ethnic strife, most of which involves fractious faiths.

"Religious tribalism" is a wellspring of trouble. American sociologist Nathan Glazer propounded that ethnicity is the most powerful force in human events. Ethnic conflicts grow from differences in race, language, economics, locale, politics, culture—and religion. Anything that divides people can spawn hostility, and religion is one of the strongest dividers. British anthropologist Desmond Morris, author of *The Naked Ape*, wrote in his 1977 book *Manwatching*, that religion is a "cultural isolating mechanism" because it "demands social separation from those who worship in a different manner. It creates sects and breeds sectarian violence."*

The faith factor is visible in much bloodshed of the 1990s. At times, the daily news seems a catalog of holy hatred: Christian Armenians and Muslim Azerbaijanis continue their slaughter in the Caucasus; fundamentalists who murdered a former Egyptian president now threaten his successor; Sikh militants in India's Punjab province kill Hindus in a drive to establish "The Land of the Pure"; Catholic islanders of East Timor languish under occupation

---

Manwatching: A Field Guide to Human Behavior (New York: Harry N. Abrams, Inc., 1977), p. 149.

by Muslim Indonesia; Sudan's never-ending war between northern Muslims and southern Christians has caused devastating famine; fundamentalists who were winning an election in Algeria turned to terrorism after the election was halted; black Muslims briefly shot their way to control of Trinidad; Christian Greeks and Muslim Turks on Cyprus still need U.N. peacekeepers to hold them apart, thirty years after plunging into combat; Buddhists in Nepal are in ferment over a new constitution that declares the mountain kingdom a Hindu state.

The United States itself has escaped major conflict, but it suffers minor wounds of religious tribalism. Various fundamentalist groups are subcultures bonded by their beliefs, some retreating from society while others wage public struggles, picket video stores, or mob abortion clinics. The most extreme U.S. tribalism involves cults living in half-secret compounds, occasionally erupting in murder.

Religion can produce individual horrors as well as ethnic warfare. Iran's *imams* (holy men) have increased the bounty offered in their *fatwa* (religious edict) demanding the assassination of a "blaspheming" author. An Ohio cultist made human sacrifices of a family of five. Iran's Shi'ites resumed hanging Baha'i believers who refuse to convert. Leaders of a Florida religious sect murdered fourteen defectors and others.

Rising fundamentalism in the 1990s has also produced tyranny, as seen in Pakistan's 1991 decree that anyone who commits "blasphemy" by insulting the Prophet Muhammad will be hanged. The country's new *sharia* code,

13

based on the Koran, requires women to be stoned to death for extramarital sex, and other offenders to have their hands or feet chopped off.

Actress Shirley MacLaine, addressing a group of newspaper editors in Baltimore in 1993, protested "the blood-drenched conflicts occurring in the name of God."

> It is becoming quite clear that religion is at the heart of so many civil wars and international struggles. People seem willing to kill, maim, torture, and die for a religious or spiritual belief which moves them to believe that their source of the divine is the only source. . . .
>
> Consider: In the name of God, a fatwa against Salman Rushdie. In the name of God, murder in the Balkans. In the name of God, the bombing of the World Trade Center. In the name of God, the siege at Waco, Texas. In the name of God, Hindus and Muslims kill each other in India. In the name of God, bloody warfare between Protestants and Catholics in Ireland. In the name of God, Shi'ites and Sunnis are at each other's throats in Iraq and Iran, as are Arabs and Jews in the Middle East. In the name of God, a doctor is murdered because he believed in a woman's right to choose. In the name of God, what is going on?

What's going on is a phenomenon the world avoids discussing, namely, the evil side of religion. Despite the universal belief that religion makes people "good," it's obvious that it makes some people commit heinous acts. The phenomenon is ancient. Although religious killing has surged to the foreground of public consciousness in the early years of this the last decade of the twentieth century, it has been recurring for centuries in one form or another. Here are just a few historical highlights:

In the eleventh century, Christian crusaders marched off to attack Muslims occupying the Holy Land, but before leaving, they massacred "the infidel among us"—Jews living in Germany. After the crusaders took Jerusalem, they slaughtered the whole population and gave thanks to God.

Some Christian groups in Europe, such as the Cathari and the Waldensians, were declared heretics, and "internal crusades" were launched against them.* When a crusader army captured the French city of Beziers in 1208, commanders asked the papal legate how to separate the town's condemned Cathari from its faithful residents. The pope's emissary replied: "Kill them all; God will know his own." It was done.

Jihads (holy wars) spread Islam as far as Spain and India. No sooner had the conquered peoples been converted than rival Muslim sects began declaring *jihads* against each other. Shi'ites, Kharijis, Azariqis, Wahhabis,

---

*The Cathari, also called Albigenses because of their concentration around Albi, France, were ascetic Christians who believed that the physical world must be shunned as evil. They defied orders from Rome to conform, and were exterminated by more than a century of crusades and persecution.

The Waldensians, or Waldenses, followed Peter Waldo, who taught that true believers must live in poverty and preach to everyone. They ignored mandates from Rome that only priests may preach. Thousands of Waldensians were killed for their beliefs, but some descendants survive today.

Mahdists, and others waged gory rebellions against the Sunni majority.*

Jews of Europe lived in peril. Christian councils forced them to wear badges of shame and reside in ghettos. Massacres happened again and again—usually after rumors spread that Jews were sacrificing Christian children in blood rituals, or that Jews were stealing host wafers from Christian churches and driving nails through them to crucify Jesus again.

The internal crusades against heretics evolved into the Inquisition, which tortured Christians into admitting unorthodoxy, then burned them for it. Later, the Inquisition focused its attention on witchcraft. Hundreds of thousands of women were tortured into confessing that they flew through the sky, changed into animals, copulated with Satan, and the like. Most were executed.

After the Reformation erupted in 1517, Europe was wracked by dozens of Catholic-Protestant wars. In France

---

*Shi'ite Muslims broke away from the Sunni mainstream in the seventh century in a dispute over who should succeed the Prophet Muhammad after his death. They backed Muhammad's son-in-law, Ali, who was rejected as successor, or caliph, and led wars against the majority.

Kharijis, or Khawarijis, were embittered followers of Ali who turned against him and eventually murdered him.

Azariqis were a fanatic splinter of the Kharijis, who declared that most other Muslims were sinners and must be killed.

Wahhabis were followers of Abd al Wahhab, a puritanical eighteenth-century holy man who preached that Islam had become worldly and sinful. Wahhabis waged two centuries of holy wars to "cleanse" Islam, and finally created the modern nation of Saudi Arabia.

Mahdists were followers of Muhammad Ahmad Ibn Assayyid, a nineteenth-century Nile Valley mystic who proclaimed himself the *Mahdi* (Divinely Guided One) sent to purify Islam. He raised an army and conquered much of Egypt and Sudan before British troops with Maxim guns destroyed the Mahdist forces.

eight wars were fought against the Protestant Huguenots, many of whom were killed in the St. Bartholomew's Day Massacre during a truce in 1572. The last bloodbath of the Reformation was the Thirty Years War in the 1600s, which killed half the population of Germany. While Catholics and Protestants were waging a century of combat against each other, both sides executed Anabaptists for the crime of double baptism. (Anabaptists held that traditional infant baptism was pointless, since babies couldn't comprehend it, so they rebaptized adult converts. But the other faiths deemed this practice a sacrilege deserving death.)

Pope Pius V typified the religious horror of that era. As Grand Inquisitor he sent troops to kill two thousand Waldensian Protestants in southern Italy. After becoming pope, he sent troops to fight Huguenot Protestants in France, telling the commander to kill all prisoners. He also launched the final crusade against Islam, sending a Christian naval armada to slaughter Muslims in the Battle of Lepanto (off the coast of Greece) in 1571. He also revived the Inquisition to torture suspected heretics. After his death, Pius V was canonized as a saint.

During the same era, elsewhere in the world, Aztecs were staging human sacrifices by the thousands in Central America, and India's Thugs, religious stranglers, sacrificed up to 20,000 victims each year for the goddess Kali before British rulers eradicated the clandestine cult in the mid-1800s.

In colonial America, New England's Puritans decreed that Quakers must be put to death as false worshipers.

Some who ventured into Massachusetts in the mid–1600s were flogged, tortured, and hanged.

Another American religious horror was Protestant-Catholic strife that killed twenty Philadelphians in 1844. It erupted because a Catholic bishop wanted Catholic children in public schools to read from Catholic scriptures, not the King James version of the Bible required by education authorities. Thousands of angry Protestants stormed a Catholic neighborhood, burning homes and churches. Martial law was declared. Troops with cannons were sent to guard Catholic churches. Then, amazingly, Protestants took cannons from sailing ships at the Philadelphia docks and fought an artillery duel with the soldiers.

After the Baha'i religion sprouted in Iran in the 1850s, the Shi'ite Muslim majority called the Baha'is infidels, and inflicted murderous persecution upon them, killing thousands.

The worst religious calamity in history was the Taiping Rebellion in China in the 1850s, which killed an estimated twenty million people. A holy man declared himself to be Jesus' younger brother and said God, his father, had instructed him to "destroy demons" and make China a theocracy. His Association of God-Worshipers mustered an army of a million followers (partly by promising them shares of the land and loot they seized). They cut a terrible swath. Eventually the rebellion was crushed by opposing armies, including one commanded by British general Charles Gordon, who was dubbed "Chinese" Gordon for his service in the Orient. (Poor Gordon was cursed by religion. After leaving China, he led an Egyptian army against Muslims waging a holy war in the Nile Valley, and was killed when the fanatics overran Khartoum.)

Christian pogroms against Jews continued into the twentieth century. Europe's nine hundred years of religious slander against Jews branded them as a despised people and set the stage for the Nazi Holocaust.

Learned people always have known that faith has a potential for horror. Mark Twain wrote: "Man is the religious animal. He is the only religious animal. He is the only animal who has the True Religion—several of them. He is the only animal who loves his neighbor as himself and cuts his throat, if his theology isn't straight. He has made a graveyard of the globe in trying his honest best to smooth his brother's path to happiness and heaven." Concurring with this view, author W. Somerset Maugham observed in *A Writer's Notebook*: "What mean and cruel things men do for the love of God." Mahatma Gandhi wrote in *Young India*: "The most heinous and the most cruel crimes of which history has record have been committed under the cover of religion or equally noble motives." Years before, Frederick the Great wrote in a 1787 letter to Voltaire: "We know the crimes that fanaticism in religion has caused." Thomas Jefferson said in 1816: "On the dogmas of religion, as distinguished from moral principles, all mankind, from the beginning of the world to this day, have been quarreling, fighting, burning and torturing one another, for abstractions unintelligible to themselves and to all others, and absolutely beyond the comprehension of the human mind." And playwright

Eugene Ionesco told *Esquire* magazine in 1974: "In the name of religion, one tortures, persecutes, builds pyres."

In 1890, when Wisconsin believers demanded worship in public schools, the state Supreme Court refused, declaring in its decision in *Weiss* v. *District Board* (1890): "There is no such source and cause of strife, quarrel, fights, malignant opposition, persecution and war, and all evil in the state, as religion. Let it once enter into our civil affairs, and our government would soon be destroyed. Let it once enter our common schools, they would be destroyed."

Clearly, in both past history and current headlines, any observer can see tragedies rooted, to one degree or another, in faith. Of course, not all ethnic conflicts have a religious aspect. For example, in the postage-stamp African nations of Rwanda and Burundi, near Lake Victoria, the Tutsis (The Tall Ones—also called Watusis) and the Hutus (The Short Ones) have massacred each other periodically for decades, out of purely tribal hostility. The slaughter surged to new heights in early 1994. However, religion is a divisive factor in so many other human hatreds that some religious figures are sickened by it. Senator John Danforth, a Republican from Missouri and an Episcopal priest, called for establishment of an international religious Security Council to intercede in such conflicts. Writing in the *Washington Post* in October 1990, he complained:

> In most if not all of the world's trouble spots, religious extremism is at the heart of the problem. In Israel, Muslims throw rocks at Jews and Jews shoot back at Muslims. In the chaos of Lebanon, religious factions

are so numerous it is difficult to keep track of them. In Northern Ireland, Catholic and Protestant Christians bomb each other as they have for decades. Hindu India and Muslim Pakistan face off against each other, offering the prospect of nuclear weapons if necessary to prove their points. . . .

All of this killing is done with the absolute certainty that God wants it so. If thine enemy offends thee, rub him out. Indeed, it is believed that to lose one's life in God's cause is to die a martyr's death and win a reward in heaven.

The senator's call was echoed in 1993 at the Parliament of the World Religions, which convened in Chicago. More than two hundred delegates from all major faiths adopted a declaration titled "Toward a Global Ethic," written by a team headed by Swiss Catholic theologian Hans Küng. It decried: "Time and again we see leaders and members of religions incite aggression, fanaticism, hate, and xenophobia—even inspire and legitimize violent and bloody conflicts. . . . We are filled with disgust. . . . We condemn aggression and hatred in the name of religion."

Rabbi Herbert Schaalman, an organizer of the parliament, said, "It's so obvious that it hurts—that so many of the things that are wrong in the world are actually due to religious conflicts." The parliament's chairman, Presbyterian David Ramage, added that, "Two-thirds of the major conflicts in the world today have religious overtones." He expressed hope that the new Global Ethic declaration will cause churches to act in joint opposition "whenever anyone kills in the name of religion in the future."

However, some groups fell into disputes before the Chicago assembly ended, and prospects for unified church action dimmed. At the end, the paradox of religious hate and murder seemed as insoluble as ever.

The chapters that follow outline this phenomenon of hatred, murder, and mayhem repeated over and over again in the name of one religion or another around the world in the 1990s.

Most of the horrors in this book are drawn from the international news wires of the Associated Press and the *New York Times,* and a few from other sources. As editor of the largest newspaper in West Virginia, I scan hundreds of reports daily at my video terminal, and I am amazed by the frequency with which religion causes people to kill each other. It is a nearly universal pattern, under-cutting the common assumption that religion makes people kind and tolerant.

A Place Once Called Yugoslavia

2

A Place Once Called Yugoslavia

Christianity broke asunder in 1054 over technicalities such as the doctrine of *filioque,* which says that the Holy Ghost comes "from the father and son." Ecclesiastics in Rome said it does; those in Constantinople said it doesn't. The issue became a power struggle over the proper interpretation of one of the main components of the Holy Trinity. The struggle ended with both sides damning the other to hell with epithets. These clerics didn't know they also were damning unlucky believers in future centuries.

This schism created a dangerous doctrinal fault-line through the Balkan region. Christians west of the line were allied with Rome and became Roman Catholic. Those to the east clung to Constantinople and became Orthodox. Thus the area north of Greece was religiously tribalized.

The region was further factionalized in the 1400s

25

when Muslim Turks seized the Balkans in their northward drive toward Vienna. As often happened after Muslim holy wars, many conquered people embraced Islam because conversion enabled them to retain their lands and privileges. Some blond, blue-eyed Slavs became Muslims and lorded over Christian peasants, who hated the turncoats nearly as much as they hated the Turkish invaders. Some Jews also lived there, fragmenting the region into four faiths. The area came to symbolize religio-ethnic turmoil.

Centuries of struggle between the Catholic Hapsburgs and Muslim Turks over the Balkans finally ended after World War I, when a kingdom was created. In 1929 it was named Yugoslavia: a patchwork of Catholic Croats and Slovenes in the northwest, Orthodox Serbs in the southeast and Muslim Bosnians in the middle—but with a mix everywhere. However, the only actual difference between Croats, Serbs, and Bosnians is their religion. As journalist Robert Kaplan wrote in *Balkan Ghosts*: "Since Croats are ethnically indistinguishable from Serbs—they come from the same Slavic race, they speak the same language, their names usually are the same—their identity rests on their Roman Catholicism."* (But the Orthodox Serbs use the Cyrillic alphabet, while Croats use Roman letters.) Similarly, columnist Anthony Lewis wrote in the *New York Times* (January 1, 1993): "It is really religion that

---

*New York: St. Martin's Press, 1993, p. 16.

The Cyrillic, or Slavic, alphabet, devised by St. Cyril in the ninth century, has many letters similar to the Roman, or Western, alphabet, while others appear to be reversed, or unfamiliar. The alphabet is used in Russia and in parts of Eastern Europe.

identifies the Serbs, Croats, and Muslims of former Yugoslavia: Eastern Orthodox, Roman Catholic, and Muslim. They are all of the same South Slav stock and speak the same language, Serbo-Croatian. But to religion have been added nationalist emotions."

The Catholics of Europe historically were for the most part anti-Semitic, which was a factor in the alliance that grew in World War II between Croats and Nazis. Hitler and Mussolini created an "independent" fascist state of Croatia, governed by Catholics of the Ustasha Party. Croatian Archbishop Alojzije Stepinac hailed it as "God's hand at work." A month after taking power, the Ustashi ordered all Jews to wear badges of shame. Then they began systematic extermination of Orthodox Serbs.

At the Jesenovac death camp, sixty-five miles southeast of Zagreb, more than 100,000 Serbs were clubbed and stabbed to death. (According to Kaplan, the Serbs contend that 750,000 were killed.) Before group executions, Croat Catholic priests led forced mass conversions of the victims, so they wouldn't go to hell as heretics. In Bosnia, Orthodox women and children were thrown off cliffs of the Dinar Alps. Jews and Gypsies also were executed. Scholar Josef Joffe dubbed the Ustashi regime "clerical fascism." (Anti-Semitism in the Balkans wasn't limited to Catholics. Kaplan writes that in neighboring Romania Orthodox members of the Legion of the Archangel Michael herded two hundred Jews into the Bucharest slaughterhouse in 1941, stripped them naked, and butchered them in meatcutting machines.)

Ustashi massacres during World War II were so gory

that they shocked even German military advisers. In retaliation, Serbs with monarchist sympathies joined the Chetnik resistance, which killed Catholics and Muslims. Other Serbs with communist inclinations joined Marshal Tito's partisan rebels and fought everyone. An estimated one million Yugoslavs died in the infighting.

During this horror, Muslims mostly sided with the Nazi Catholics. War historian John Keegan writes that the Waffen S.S., the special army of Nazi chief Heinrich Himmler, created a Slav division "composed of that strange minority of Serbian Muslims, the descendants of those Christian mountaineers forcibly converted to Islam by the Turks in the Middle Ages. . . . The Bosnians, whose hatred for the Christian Serbs was bitter and mutual . . . declared themselves more than ready to take on Tito's men, their traditional religious enemies." The Muslim Nazi soldiers "wore the fez, with the S.S. runes, and were led in prayer by regimental imams," he says. "Himmler had secured the services of the Grand Mufti of Jerusalem as overseer of the division's religious practices."* The Grand Mufti was the chief arbiter of Islamic law. The fez hat, the well-known inverted flower pot, symbolized Turkish influence, while the mystical rune symbols, from an ancient Germanic language, symbolized Teutonic power.

Keegan says the Muslim division was unmanageable and refused "to operate outside its own area, where it confined itself chiefly to massacring and pillaging the defenseless Christians."

Waffen SS: The Asphalt Soldiers (New York: Balantine Books, 1970), p. 104.

U.S. bomber pilots conducting raids over the Balkans were warned to hide their G.I. dogtags if they were shot down. The tags were stamped P for Protestant, C for Catholic, or H for Hebrew—any of which might prove fatal, depending on the faith of armed groups encountered. Only with the partisan Communists were downed fliers of all types safe.

After Tito triumphed and created a communist state, he imprisoned Archbishop Stepinac as a war criminal and jailed many Catholic priests who had abetted the Ustashi executions. Pope Pius XII made Stepinac a cardinal in confinement.

The iron fist of the communist state suppressed Yugoslavia's religious tribalism for four decades. Cities such as Sarajevo became known as bastions of tolerance where people of all faiths lived and worked together. But the divisions were lying dormant, like viruses lodged in tissue. After European Communism collapsed, the viruses grew and Yugoslavia disintegrated in bloodshed.

Ethnic ferment rose in 1990. Pope John Paul II endorsed the "legitimate aspirations" of Catholic Croats and Slovenes wanting to break away from Yugoslavia. In 1991, Slovenia and Croatia declared independence from the Orthodox-Muslim South, triggering war with the Yugoslav army and among various paramilitary groups. Jews weren't left out of the trouble. Bombs wrecked Jewish facilities in Zagreb, the capital of Croatia. Serbs soon gave up on Slovenia, the northernmost sector, but about 10,000 were killed in Croatia before an uneasy calm returned.

The Vatican was first to recognize the two new Catholic nations.

Then in 1992, Muslims in Bosnia-Herzegovina voted for independence, precipitating the all-out religious war that stunned the world. Bosnian Serbs protested that the "Islamic fundamentalists" and "Khomeinis" planned a theocracy in which women would be forced to wear veils. Scant evidence existed for this, but the Eastern Orthodox Christians launched armed resistance, supported by neighboring Serbia. The rebels likened themselves to Orthodox heroes who died in the Battle of Kosovo in 1389 in a futile attempt to stop the Muslim northward advance. "We are still fighting to keep Islam from spreading into the heart of Europe," said Dusan Simic, president of the city council at Pristina, capital of the southern province of Kosovo. Many Orthodox soldiers wore uniform patches commemorating the six-century-old Battle of Kosovo.

Serbian President Slobodan Milosevic called for the "ethnic cleansing" of Bosnia—in other words, the eradication of Muslims and Catholics. The cleansing became a new holocaust: Orthodox troops seized towns, dragged Muslims from their homes, and killed them or shipped them to detention camps. At Prijedor, near Bosnia's northwest border, Muslim prisoners were forced to bow to Mecca, then were clubbed with pipes. At Koritnik, soldiers dropped grenades into a basement containing Muslim families and joked that the screams sounded "just like a mosque." Muslim leader Abdullah Hodzic said the troops destroyed seven hundred mosques. At one they rolled a mullah in his prayer rug in front of worshipers, set the rug afire, then shot the worshipers. United Nations peacekeepers found bodies in some mosques. At the city of Foca, thirty miles southeast of Sarajevo, thirteen mosques were dynamited.

Western observers likened the "ethnic cleansing" of Muslims to the Nazi extermination of Jews in World War II. In 1992, the *Economist* of London commented: "When all the Muslims of some Bosnian town are rounded up and led away, to the jeers of their Christian neighbors, nobody with a modicum of mercy or memory can look the other way. Although it is not Belsen* in Bosnia, and will probably never be, it is certainly beyond *Kristallnacht.*†"

Croatia was drawn into the war, temporarily supporting the Muslims. Croats destroyed Orthodox churches. Serbs destroyed Catholic churches. Atrocities occurred on all sides: Orthodox troops systematically raped Muslim women; and in the siege of Sarajevo, Orthodox snipers picked off Muslim children, hitting many in the head. At one detention camp, crosses were cut into the chests of Muslim men. At a Serb camp at Trnopolje, in northwest Bosnia, two hundred Muslim prisoners were loaded into trucks, supposedly to be hauled to Muslim territory. But the trucks halted at an isolated spot, where the prisoners were massacred.

Most of the world condemned Serbia as the aggressor—yet the Serbs saw themselves as victims. Four

---

*One of the infamous Nazi death camps.

†The night of terror in 1938 when Nazi Brown Shirts destroyed Jewish-owned businesses in Germany.

An Orthodox church lies in ruins in the Croatian town of Vukovar. (Josef Koudelka/Magnum Photos)

American Orthodox bishops, including the Serbian Orthodox prelate of the Eastern United States, issued a statement in April 1993 declaring, in part:

> Still fresh in the minds of the Serbs is the memory of the genocide carried out against them in Croatia and Bosnia only a generation ago. More than 750,000 Serbs were murdered in the name of an ethnically and religiously pure Croatia. Bosnian Muslims joined the Croatians in carrying out this program of "ethnic cleansing" only comparable to the Jewish and Armenian holocausts.
>
> Serbs in Croatia and Bosnia have good reason to believe that they will not be able to live as equal citizens in these newly "independent" countries. In Croatia, Serbs have been relegated to second-class citizens. . . . More than 300 Serbian churches and cultural monuments, including the Jesenovac concentration camp (the Auschwitz for Serbs) have been desecrated or destroyed, and most Serbian Orthodox bishops and priests have been forced to leave. . . .
>
> In Bosnia, Chairman Alija Izetbegovic has declared that his goal is the creation of an Islamic fundamentalist state. As he recently said, "There can be no peace and no coexistence between Islamic faith and non-Islamic faith and non-Islamic social and political institutions."*

After a period as allies, Muslim and Croat militias began killing each other. Catholic units stormed Muslim

---

*Pittsburgh Post-Gazette, April 23, 1993.

U.N. troops help a wounded Bosnian woman in central Sarajevo. (Paul Lowe/Magnum Photos)

towns, and Muslim brigades retaliated against Croat civilians. At Stupni Do, a Bosnian mountain village about a dozen miles north of Sarajevo, Croat troops hacked and clubbed all civilians to death, including children; burned their bodies; and destroyed the town. At Uzdol, in central Bosnia in September 1993, one hundred Muslim troops massacred thirty-five Catholics including a thirteen-year-old girl.

Then Croats and Muslims negotiated a truce in 1994 and became allies again. Croatian newspapers, which had printed cartoons of Muslim leader Izetbegovic as a cross-eating monster, began depicting him as a kindly comrade. "We could become schizophrenic from changes like these," Zagreb University psychologist Mirjana Krizmanic remarked.

After the first year of fighting, Bosnian authorities estimated the death toll at 200,000. About three million people had fled as refugees. The center of the former Yugoslavia was devastated, just as Lebanon had been wrecked by religious tribal war a decade earlier. For example, at the north-central Bosnian industrial city of Banja Luka, Orthodox militants obliterated history by blowing up two Muslim mosques built in the 1500s.

About one thousand volunteer *mujahideen* (holy warriors) from various Muslim countries came to Bosnia to help the embattled Muslims, but their fanaticism soon became a problem. They killed a U.N. relief worker and a Danish truck driver, causing a temporary halt in deliveries of food to desperate civilians.

The U.N. Security Council voted unanimously to

A Bosnian militiaman looks back at the body of a young man killed by sniper fire after one of many cease-fires in Sarajevo. (AP/Wide World Photos)

establish a war crimes court, the first since the Nuremberg tribunal which tried Nazis after World War II. The U.S. State Department listed war criminals and cited Serbian President Milosevic for failure to prevent atrocities. The World Court at the Hague ruled that genocide was in progress. According to Associated Press reporter Maud Beelman (April 10, 1994), the first convicted war criminal was Serb soldier Borislav Herak, who was sentenced to death for raping several Muslim women prisoners, then taking them to a mountainside and cutting their throats. From his cell, he said his Orthodox commanders "told us that whoever doesn't wear a cross doesn't belong to us and should be killed."

In August 1994, a Serb deserter told the *New York Times* that he witnessed the execution of an estimated 3,000 Muslims at a detainment camp called Susica, northwest of Sarajevo. The camp, which operated only four months in 1992, was in a valley near the mining city of Vlasenica. The *Times* said Vlasenica formerly contained 18,699 Muslims, but all were driven out or killed through "ethnic cleansing."

Life for civilians in Bosnia's besieged cities was hideous. People attempted to work amid sniper fire and mortar attacks. Death in the streets was a daily horror. Often families crouched in basements without food, water, electricity, or heat. In Gorazde, thirty miles east of Sarajevo, men slipped through the siege lines at night and climbed to snowy mountains to bring food back to their families. Several froze on the trail, which was soon called "the road of white death." In Srebrenica, near the eastern border with Serbia, when U.N. trucks evacuated 4,300

Anxious Croatians await the all-clear signal in an underground bomb shelter during an air-raid alarm in Zagreb. (Reuters/Bettmann)

Muslim survivors, a dozen people were crushed in the panicky stampede to freedom. In Mostar, starving Muslims caught between Catholic and Orthodox attackers watched their historic city blasted to rubble. They tied old tires onto the town's stone arch bridge, built in 1557, in a futile attempt to deflect mortar shells. After the bridge fell, Muslims had to run across a temporary swinging bridge through sniper fire to obtain water.

The most widely publicized siege victims were those in Sarajevo, who saw their friends and relatives killed day after day in the streets. Twelve-year-old Zlata Filipovic reduced Western readers to tears in 1994 when her intelligent, moving, and tragic daily diary was published. Her entry for May 7, 1992, shows the horror this little girl had to endure: "Today a shell fell on the park in front of my house, the park where I used to play and sit with my girlfriends. A lot of people were hurt, and Nina is dead. A piece of shrapnel lodged in her brain and she died. She was such a sweet, nice little girl. We went to kindergarten together."[*]

An American sportswriter who had covered the 1984 Winter Olympics at Sarajevo returned to the Olympic site in 1994, and was sickened. He saw bodies of sniper victims lying in the streets and behind the wheels of crashed cars. He saw the burned hulks of Olympic hotels torched by Serb artillery units as they withdrew from hill positions after U.S. President Clinton threatened air strikes against them. Death and ruin were everywhere.

---

[*]*Zlata's Diary: A Child's Life in Sarajevo* (New York: Viking Penguin, 1994).

A poignant incident involved a couple sometimes called "Romeo and Juliet in Sarajevo." A young Orthodox Serb man, Bosko Brkic, and a Muslim girl, Admira Ismic, had been high school sweethearts and wanted to marry, despite religious barriers. While he was away for compulsory military training, she wrote to him: "My dear love. . . . Just a little bit of time is left until we are together. After that, absolutely nothing can separate us." When the war erupted, Bosko wouldn't join Orthodox troops killing Admira's relatives, nor would he join Muslim units killing his own relatives. So the couple tried to escape from Sarajevo. They attempted to run across a bridge that was under sniper fire from both sides. They made it two-thirds of the way, when both were hit. He died instantly. She crawled to him and then died. Their entwined bodies lay on the bridge for six days before they could be removed.

When a Serb mortar bomb killed seventy people in Sarajevo's marketplace in 1994, Western leaders threatened massive retaliation against Serbs, and some of the sieges eased. But daily killing continued in other sectors.

To outsiders, the carnage seemed senseless—a mindless butchery among former neighbors who are identical except for their religion. After Vukovar was shattered by a battle between Serbs and Croats, a news reporter asked Serbian college student Steven Curcija why the groups were fighting. "The difference is just the church we go to," the youth replied.

The power of religious labels was visible in 1994 when Iran—which has no connection to Bosnia except their common Islamic faith—violated a U.N. embargo by air-

Mourners who gather at Lion's Cemetery in Sarajevo to bury their dead, duck for cover as mortars explode near the funeral service. (AP/Wide World Photos)

lifting munitions and war supplies to the embattled Muslims. Within days the Bosnians launched a fierce counter-offensive.

Religious scholar Paul Mojzes calls the Yugoslavia horror "ethnoreligious warfare." In his 1994 book, he said posters proclaiming that "God Protects Croatia" dotted the Catholic state. Croats see each Serb assault "as an advance of Orthodoxy in a westward direction," he wrote, adding, "The Roman Catholic Church glorifies Croat history and virtues, and promotes the notion that Catholic Croatia forms Western Christendom's most important bulwark against the hordes from the East."*

Ironically, religion had lost much of its potency in Yugoslavia before the society fractured along religious lines. One poll in the early 1990s indicated that only 17 percent of Bosnians still deemed themselves devout. Yet when independence-seeking Muslims adopted Islamic symbols, it triggered paranoia among neighbors of Christian background. Writing in the *New York Review of Books*, Michael Ignatieff related: "The Serbs took one look at the green banners and crescents of the Muslim parties and believed that independence, under Muslim rule, delivered them up to ethnic majority tyranny."† Mojzes noted that a typical Croat is casual about church attendance. "Yet, ironically and tragically, he wears his decidedly vague Roman Catholic identity as a badge of loyalty for which, curiously, he is willing both to kill and to die.

Yugoslavia Inferno: Ethnoreligious Warfare in the Balkans (New York: Continuum, 1994).

†*The New York Review of Books*, April 21, 1994, p. 4.

Paradoxically, the current Balkan wars are religious wars fought by irreligious people."*

Jim Wright of Texas, former speaker of the U.S. House of Representatives, wrote in 1994 that he was baffled by the "demonic cruelties" of the Catholic-Orthodox-Muslim war in Yugoslavia. In the *Fort Worth Star-Telegram*, he said: "The hate that a religious war generates seems to burn with a special intensity. So little can we understand of it. This war is not about land or race or political philosophy. It is about religion. It is also about vengeance and the insatiable, self-perpetuating thirst to settle old scores. Each new act of retributive cruelty fuels the lust among its victims' kin to find satisfaction in a counteratrocity. . . .

"The Slavs are of the same race. They look alike, live alike, talk the same language, bleed the same color. Only their religion divides them. And that may be history's greatest irony. We hate in the name of what should teach us to love."

The Christian Century (book excerpt), June 15–22, 1994, p. 609.

The destruction of a residential community in Vukovar, Croatia. (Josef Koudelka/Magnum Photos)

India

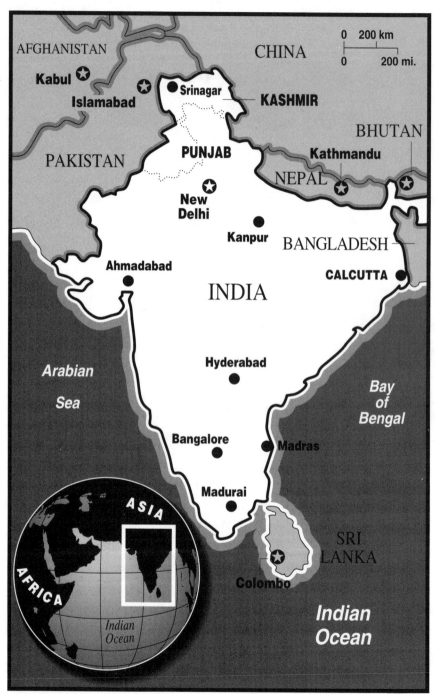

3

India

India's eternal religious hatreds boiled in many locales during the 1990s, especially at three flashpoints: In Kashmir, Muslims and Hindus killed each other with new fury. In Punjab, Sikhs continued killing Hindus in an attempt to establish "The Land of the Pure." And at the north-central town of Ayodhya, 300 miles southeast of New Delhi, a dispute over a mythical holy site loosed a national bloodbath.

The Ayodhya spot is a hilltop where Muslims built a mosque in the 1500s. Hindus contend that their god Rama was born on that hilltop 900,000 years ago (or 5,000 years ago, depending on the priest consulted). Fighting over the site has recurred for centuries, with each side claiming many martyrs.

In 1949, Hindu priests smuggled an idol of Rama into

the mosque, and the government padlocked it to avert a massacre. Muslims and Hindus filed lawsuits, and the litigation continued for nearly four decades.

In 1989, the World Hindu Council called for forceful seizure of the hilltop and replacement of the mosque with a Rama temple. The secular government sent troops to Ayodhya to keep the peace.

In 1990, the Hindu fundamentalist Bharatiya Janata political party and other groups called for a pilgrimage to Ayodhya. More than 100,000 believers swarmed to the town. A Hindu princess arrived in a caravan of three hundred trucks. About 20,000 soldiers formed a ring around the mosque, rifles at the ready. Violent clashes occurred day after day. More than 100 pilgrims were shot and 80,000 were arrested. Hindus poured kerosene on a Muslim man and burned him alive. About 200 Hindu youths broke through the military line and planted flags on the mosque.

The Ayodhya drama caused Hindu-Muslim riots in cities throughout India. More than 1,000 people were stabbed, clubbed, stoned, or burned to death. The resulting political uproar caused the government of Prime Minister V.P. Singh to fall.

The following year the Bharatiya Janata party ran on an election platform that called for destroying the Ayodhya mosque. The party drew enormous support, becoming the second largest in India.

In 1992, fundamentalists called for a second pilgrimage: this time 300,000 converged on Ayodhya. Troops couldn't stop the ocean of zealots: thousands with crowbars, pickaxes, and other instruments mobbed the mosque

Thousands of Hindu fundamentalists converge on the entrance to the Babri Mosque in Ayodhya, India, in 1990 in an unsuccessful attempt to destroy it and construct a Hindu temple of their own on the same site. (AP/Wide World Photos)

In 1992, Hindu fundamentalists return to the Babri Mosque. This time they were successful in overwhelming Muslim resistance and destroying the structure. (Reuters/Bettmann)

and ripped it to rubble. Immediately they began building a Rama shrine in its place.

The mosque's destruction triggered a national convulsion that killed more than 2,000 people. Riots and massacres occurred in scores of cities. Muslim mobs armed with hatchets, pipes, knives, and homemade bombs raged through the streets killing Hindus. At the city of Nuh, fifty miles north of New Delhi, they ransacked ten Hindu temples, shouting "Kill the Hindu dog." Hindus retaliated by throwing fiery gasoline-soaked rags into Muslim homes, starting conflagrations. Bombay had nine days of nonstop riots. A pall of smoke hung over the city. In Tanda, east of Kanpur, a Muslim milkman carrying two heavy cans was stabbed in the back by Muslims who mistook him for a Hindu.

India's neutral government banned the Bharatiya Janata party and arrested its leaders. Also banned were fundamentalist religious councils (but India's Supreme Court later struck down the ban).

Across the border in Pakistan, enraged Muslims destroyed scores of Hindu temples and attacked Hindu homes and shops. Muslim sheiks declared a *jihad* against India.

Two months later, numerous bombs were detonated in Bombay, killing hundreds. Some of them hit the headquarters of Hindu groups, evidently in retaliation for the mosque attack.

Since Hinduism has 330 million gods,* all this might

*Alain Danielou, *Hindu Polytheism* (New York: Pantheon Books, 1964), p. 84.

seem excessive concern over the supposed birthplace of just one of them. However, the concern obviously was enough to spark the killing.

Not all Indians feel the violent passions of the fundamentalists. During the national spasm over the mosque, some university professors and students spoke out. Hari Kumar, a Hindu graduate student at Delhi University, said his fellow Hindus "are not being rational people." Professor Tahir Mahmood of the Indian Institute of Islamic Studies likened the Hindu attackers to Nazis who smashed Jewish synagogues, shops, and homes on *Kristallnacht* in 1938.

*   *   *

Other religious conflicts are interminable in India. A gory one exists in the northwest Punjab province, where Sikhs want to break away and establish a theocracy called Khalistan (Land of the Pure). To this end, Sikh militants often massacre Hindu families and shoot up Hindu weddings. The conflict reached its worst in 1984 when Sikhs assassinated Prime Minister Indira Gandhi. Hindus retaliated with grotesque massacres that killed 5,000 Sikhs in three days.

In 1985, Sikh militants planted a bomb on an Air India jet that exploded off the coast of Ireland, killing all 329 aboard. One of the terrorists was finally caught in 1992.

The Punjab conflict leveled off in the 1990s, drawing little world attention. News summaries said there were

4,200 religious killings in Punjab in 1991 and 3,800 in 1992—a routine death rate scarcely noticed by the Western media: Sikh separatists stopped two trains one day and killed 74 Hindus. Six months later, they stopped another train and killed 55. On another occasion, they stopped a bus and shot 16 Hindus. When a Hindu festival was held at the town of Ruderpur, a rice farming town 140 miles northeast of New Delhi, bombs exploded and 40 people were killed. In the fall of 1993, a Sikh car bomb in India's capital of New Delhi killed eight. In early 1994, another bomb exploded in a New Delhi movie theater, wounding 18.

Occasionally, the militants even killed fellow Sikhs who failed to support the terrorism.

In 1994, two Sikh groups offered $483,000 bounty to anyone who would assassinate Pakistani author Sadiq Hussain, on grounds that his book, *The History of the Holy Warriors*, relating the history of Sikhism, "blasphemed" founders of the religion. Posters announcing the reward were posted in Sikh shrines around Punjab. A Sikh leader asked Pakistani Prime Minister Benazir Bhutto to confiscate all copies of the book, calling it "nothing but a bundle of lies."

The turbaned, whiskered Sikhs are a warrior clan who branched off from Hinduism five hundred years ago. But the kinship of the two faiths doesn't reduce hostilities between them. Year after year, a dreadful lesson about religion is seen in Punjab, where murder is employed to advance "the land of the pure."

At least 76 people were killed and 41 wounded when Sikh militants attacked two trains in the state of Punjab. (The Bettmann Archive)

The third India flashpoint is the northwestern Kashmir province, a disputed territory between India and Pakistan. Here Hindu-Muslim conflict has killed untold thousands during the past half-century.

When British rulers prepared to set India free in 1947, they saw that religious hatreds would explode as soon as their military power departed. To control the animosity, Britain established two nations: India for Hindus and Pakistan for Muslims. But the partition didn't avert tragedy. Up to one million people died in bloody clashes as Muslims rushed to Pakistan and Hindus rushed to India. (It was a tragic irony that Mahatma Gandhi, the "Great Soul" of nonviolence, won India's liberation, which then loosed a religious bloodbath. Gandhi himself was assassinated by a militant Hindu who thought Gandhi favored the Muslims.)

Kashmir was made part of India, although it has a Muslim majority. Ever since, Muslim attempts to sever Kashmir from India have caused bloodshed. Three times— in 1948, in 1965, and in 1971—India and Pakistan fought border wars over the province. Now, each administers a segment, separated by a cease-fire line.

In 1989, Muslim militants in the Indian-controlled sector began another push for separation. As many as 800,000 Muslims marched at one time, and many were chanting "We are ready for holy war." Indian troops tried to quell the rebellion, but as the struggle dragged on during the next six years, thousands died. Again and again, militants threw grenades or firebombs, and Hindu soldiers replied with volleys, leaving dozens of bodies in streets.

Indian troops are called to the Kashmir city of Srinagar to stop rioting between Muslims and Hindus at the Hazaratbal Mosque. (AP/Wide World Photos)

Fervent Muslim youths ravaged liquor stores, movie theaters, video rental shops, and beauty parlors in Kashmir to enforce religious puritanism.

The uprising produced a bizarre siege at Srinagar, the Kashmir capital, in 1993. Sixty Muslims with automatic weapons barricaded themselves inside the region's holiest place, the white marble Hazaratbal Mosque, to defend its holiest relic, a whisker from Muhammad's beard, carefully housed in a satin bag. The Muslims said they were protecting the whisker from Hindus. But Hindu authorities feared that the militants planned to carry the whisker through the province to incite Muslims to rebellion.

While troops surrounded the mosque, Muslims outside gathered in mobs. Soldiers fired into the crowds, killing 60. After a month, the militants came out of the mosque peacefully, but ambushes, fires, and riots continued throughout Kashmir.

For example, thinking they were being attacked, Hindu soldiers at the town of Kupwara opened fire in early 1994, killing 18 Muslims at a market. Soon thereafter, militants ambushed a patrol, and the surviving soldiers, in a fit of rage, stormed nearby homes, killing many residents.

In the same year, Indian authorities disclosed that 9,000 people had died in the five-year uprising. But a record maintained by Kashmiri journalists and professionals put the toll nearer to 20,000. (Hindu-Muslim hatred in Kashmir often defies its own rather bizarre logic: During the 1989 wave of Muslim riots over Salman Rushdie's novel

The Satanic Verses, Kashmiri Muslims attacked a Hindu temple—even though the author came from a Muslim family!)

Both India and Pakistan now possess nuclear weapons. American diplomats have expressed apprehension that if a fourth border war is fought over Kashmir, it might be the world's first thermonuclear religious war.

* * *

In addition to the major conflicts noted above, random bursts of fatal faith erupt constantly throughout India. For example, in the western city of Ahmadabad, Muslims attacked a Hindu religious procession in 1992. It triggered two days of rioting with daggers, rocks, pipes, and other crude weapons, which killed nine. When police shot into the mobs, five more died.

Religious violence is so ingrained in India that the Hindi language has a special word for it, *dharmiklarai* (religious fight). The word is used daily. The nation has many enlightened, educated people, but they can't restrain the destructive force of the simplistic, narrow-minded believers in their midst.

Ulster (Northern Ireland)

Atlantic
Ocean

UNITED
KINGDOM

SCOTLAND

North
Sea

Edinburgh

NORTHERN
IRELAND
Belfast

ENGLAND

Baile Átha
Cliath
(Dublin)

Irish
Sea

Liverpool

GREAT
BRITAIN

Limerick

IRELAND

WALES

Birmingham

Cork

Cardiff

London

Celtic Sea

Bristol

Orkney
Islands

EUROPE

AFRICA

Plymouth

English Channel

FRANCE

0   100 km

0   100 mi.

Bill Pitzer- PITZO*Graphics*

4

Ulster (Northern Ireland)

Europe's historic Wars of Religion between Catholics and Protestants ended three centuries ago—except in Northern Ireland. There the conflict never stopped: killing based on religious identity is as cruel today as in the 1500s. Consider this one-week sequence in 1993: After secret Protestant terror squads of the Ulster Defense Association (UDA) assassinated three Catholics in mid-October, the chief Catholic terror group, the furtive Irish Republican Army (IRA), retaliated on October 23. It sent a young assassin with a plastic explosive to a Belfast fish shop under the headquarters of the outlawed UDA. The bomb exploded prematurely, killing the IRA agent and nine Protestants, including a seven-year-old girl.

Protestant paramilitaries vowed "terrible vengeance"—and delivered it. That same night, UDA killers

The funeral cortege of three victims passes by the remains of a fish market bombed by IRA terrorists. (Bettmann)

shot a Catholic fast-food deliverer. Two days later, they killed a seventy-two-year-old Catholic man. The following day, they killed two Catholic trash-haulers. Two days later, they shot dead two Catholic brothers who were at home watching television. A week after the bombing, on Halloween, Protestant gunmen entered a pub in the Catholic village of Greysteel. One shouted "Trick or treat!" and they opened fire with automatic weapons, killing seven. The death toll for the week was 23.

Subsequently, Catholic "hit men" counterattacked, picking off British soldiers with sniper fire, planting more bombs in Protestant locales, and setting Protestant stores afire. Protestant agents replied by killing a man and a teen-ager at a taxi office. By year's end, murders in a quarter-century of Ulster strife had passed 3,200.

The troubles in Northern Ireland are political, economic, cultural, and historic, but fervent if not virulent religious identity is what keeps the hate alive. It dictates which side an Ulster resident supports in a 400-year-old feud. A writer friend of mine says that "Irish amnesia" is a condition of people "who have forgotten everything but their grudges." Religious tribalism is what prevents ancient Ulster grudges from fading.

Those feuds stem from centuries of English encroachment. Starting in the 1100s, English monarchs attempted intermittently to subjugate the green island. After Henry VIII broke with the church of Rome in the 1500s, a religious dimension was added: English Protestants were trying to conquer Irish Catholics. Elizabeth I completed the seizure of Ireland, but rebellions were frequent. Then

James I took a fateful step in 1609 that doomed Northern Ireland to endless religious conflict. To reward Scottish and English commanders who had defeated the Irish, and to establish a secure Protestant settlement, James confiscated choice land in the northeastern Ulster region and gave it to his officers and other Protestants. The former owners were driven into the hills, where life was meager. Eventually, some crept back to become field hands on the estates they once owned. Their bitterness was deep as most Catholics remained in the hills. Today, some say sardonically: "The Protestants got the land. We got the view."

Throughout the whole island, England tried to suppress recurring Irish uprisings. Meanwhile, in England, fanatical Puritans under Oliver Cromwell temporarily seized power from King Charles I, spelling worse trouble for the Irish. Cromwell brought his hymn-singing, Psalm-saying Protestant army to Ireland and massacred Catholics and their priests, calling the slaughter "a righteous judgment of God."

In the 1700s, the Penal Laws banned Catholicism and expelled priests. Troops hunted Irish Catholics who persisted in secret worship. In the 1800s, the right to worship openly was restored, but Catholics were required to pay tithes to the Anglican Church. This triggered the brief Tithe War in which both Catholics and Protestants committed atrocities.

Finally, in the aftermath of World War I, another Catholic uprising forced England to set Ireland free. But Protestants in six northern counties around Belfast—occupying lands their ancestors usurped from Catholics three centuries before—panicked at the prospect of living under a "papist" government. They voted to remain part of Great Britain, thus becoming the separate state of Northern Ireland in 1921. The state often is called Ulster, after the ancient Irish district that occupied a slightly larger territory.

Outnumbered, Catholics in Ulster, who were barely second-class citizens living in poverty, clamored for equality. In the 1950s, the clandestine IRA began terrorism in an attempt to force unification of all Ireland. Catholic riots in 1968 and 1969 brought Protestant reprisals with guns, bombs, and burnings. IRA sabotage increased, and British troops were sent in.

Ever since, Northern Ireland has seethed with half-suppressed civil war. Barricades, military patrols, barbed wire, and sentry posts keep the capital of Belfast separated into religious compounds. Protestants and Catholics live in segregated neighborhoods, afraid to venture into "enemy" territory. At connecting streets where the neighborhoods meet, violence is common. Sniper fire cracked across these lines at night until authorities erected twenty-foot "peace walls." Despite all the security efforts, murders never seem to cease.

I went to Belfast in 1986 with twenty other newspaper editors on a study mission. It was a gripping experience. Soldiers with machine guns patroled airport corridors while security guards combed every item in our luggage. The bus to our hotel passed through military checkpoints like a war zone. British Governor Tom King told us that "security is the biggest industry we've got," providing more jobs than any other business. At that time, tiny Ulster, with only 1.5 million people, had 12,767 police officers and 15,573 soldiers.

The day before our arrival, an IRA bomb that had been wired to a car's ignition killed an eighteen-year-old army reservist and mangled the face of his teenage fiancee who was seated beside him. As we arrived, doctors were trying to save her from blindness, and Protestant ministers were conducting the youth's funeral in the church where they had planned to marry.

Belfast officials told us proudly that Catholic-Protestant violence had dwindled to its lowest level. They gave us a report showing that incidents declined in 1985 to merely 54 assassinations, 916 woundings, 148 explosions, 237 shooting episodes, 522 arrests on terrorism charges, 175 gun seizures, confiscation of 3.3 tons of explosives, and 31 "kneecappings," the grotesque means by which secret groups command authority in ghettos.

Some of us slipped into the Free Presbyterian Church to hear a sermon by the Rev. Ian Paisley, the demagogue of militant Protestants. He called the Catholic mass "a blasphemy and a deceit." He sneered at "bachelor priests" and derided Catholicism as "un-Christian." (Paisley is so popular among Ulster's Protestants that he's elected repeatedly to the European Parliament. When Pope John Paul II addressed the parliament at Strasbourg in 1988, Paisley screamed at him and waved a sign labeling the pope the anti-Christ. Guards ejected him.)

Some of us visited the barricaded headquarters of Sinn Fein, the Catholic political party allied with the IRA. Sitting

A British soldier sights his rifle as his armored vehicle is driven past an image of the Virgin Mary. (Bettmann)

in rooms with bulletproof glass windows, Sinn Fein leaders told us they were marked for death by Protestant "murder gangs." They recited horror stories of Catholic children killed by British troops. (While Protestants voiced their antipathy in religious terms, the Catholic activists spoke only of political ferment against the British.) Twice-jailed leader Martin McGuinness said Ireland was the first colony seized by England in its centuries of empire-building, "and our small country is the last place they still have a toehold."

The Sinn Fein leaders seemed earnest and reasonable—but their publications were hideous. Its magazines proudly printed photographs of the "armed struggle" by the IRA. The pictures showed a murdered Protestant professor lying on a sidewalk outside his college; a soldier riddled by automatic rifle fire as he walked to his home; a policeman machine gunned in his car in a roadside ambush; a twenty-five-year-old IRA member executed as a suspected turncoat; and two soldiers killed by a bomb hidden in a culvert. One magazine boasted of sixty-two killings, fire-bombings, and murder attempts in a four-month period. One item said the killing of a soldier raised IRA morale. Editorials crowed that the IRA "will fight on."

I had a dizzy sense of being in a madhouse, where horrors are deemed noble, or at least normal.

After our group of journalists had left Ulster, the horror continued as usual, with tit-for-tat murders occurring almost weekly. In 1990, the IRA tried a new tactic: gunmen held a family hostage and forced the father to drive a bomb-rigged car into a British target street. The blast killed the father and six soldiers.

Car bombs are a typical and highly destructive form of religious terrorism in Northern Ireland. (© Mike Sheil/International Stock Photo)

In 1992, a Protestant disguised as a journalist entered the Sinn Fein headquarters where I had sat six years earlier. He pulled out a hidden shotgun and killed three people. About the same time, Catholic terrorists blew up a van and killed eight Protestants; Ulster Freedom Fighters retaliated by shooting five Catholics at a Belfast betting shop.

In the same year, a huge IRA bomb caused $500 million damage to the heart of London's financial district. A year later, with some of the repairs still unfinished, a second bomb in the same district caused even more damage.

In 1994, Irish Catholic terrorists lobbed mortars at London's Heathrow Airport, while Protestant terrorists in Belfast fired rockets and bullets at the Sinn Fein office I had visited.

In mid-1994, as England and France prepared to open the $15 billion "chunnel" under the English Channel, strict security measures were imposed out of fear that an IRA bomb might trap thousands of travelers beneath the sea. Not long after the tunnel opened, two Protestant gunmen of the Ulster Volunteer Force entered a rural pub where twenty-five Catholics were watching a telecast of Ireland's soccer team playing in the World Cup games. The assassins opened fire, killing six and wounding five.

Ironically, amid the madness of religious killings, Ulster remains one of the loveliest areas of the British Isles. It's as far north as Hudson Bay, yet eternally green and mild, thanks to warm water of the Gulf Stream. Belfast is backed by smooth, treeless mountains that loom like great loaves of bread. The city is filled with charming, ornate Victorian buildings. The people are jovial and affectionate, and, surprisingly enough, except for the terrorism, the city has one of the world's lowest crime rates.

"The Troubles," as they are called, demonstrate how religion can perpetuate historic hostilities. If today's Ulster residents weren't Catholic or Protestant, they would have no reason to belong to one camp and hate the other. A young person growing up in Belfast wouldn't identify with either the victims or the victors in a 1609 land-grab, if religious heritage and conditioning didn't dictate the sides. Ulster's people are alike in appearance, language, dress, and habits. Their ancient feud would have faded long ago through social intermingling and intermarriage, had not church labels kept them segregated. The estrangement keeps old wounds fresh.

The poet Yeats wrote of the "terrible beauty"* that haunts the soul "wherever green is worn."

> Out of Ireland we have come,
> Great hatred, little room,
> Maimed us at the start.
> I carry from my mother's womb
> A fanatic's heart.†

*from "Easter 1916"
†from "Remorse for Intemperate Speech"

A body lies in a West Belfast street after Protestant Loyalists attacked a group of workers. (AP/Wide World Photos)

Sudan

Bill Pitzer- PITZO*Graphics*

5

Sudan

The deadliest religious conflict of the 1990s was also the worst of the 1980s, the 1970s, the 1960s, and the 1950s.

Perhaps two million people have died in Sudan's forty-year intermittent war between Muslims in the north and Christians and animists* in the south. The world has paid scant attention to this long-running horror in which famine is used as a weapon of extermination. But its death toll exceeds that of all other current hostilities.

In the mid-1990s it seems possible that "ethnic cleansing" may destroy the Christian and animist culture, leaving survivors subjugated in a Muslim theocracy. The United Nations, the United States, and humanitarian groups all condemn the persecution, but to little avail.

---

*The primitive belief that natural objects and forces have souls.

A central issue in the conflict is whether the *shariá*—the Islamic code under which thieves have their hands chopped off, lovers are stoned to death, and drinkers are publicly flogged—will be imposed on non-Muslims. Other religious, ethnic, and tribal factors also fuel the trouble that goes back more than a dozen centuries.

Sudan, Africa's largest nation, encompasses the upper Nile region south of Egypt. In ancient times, Arab slave traders invaded the deep south to seize captives. After Islam was born in the seventh century, Arab incursions brought the new faith to the northern sector around Khartoum, but not to the remote tribal south.

British colonialism came to Sudan in the 1890s as a result of a holy war. A Muslim mystic named Muhammad Ahmad said he was the prophesied *Mahdi* (divinely guided one) destined to lead a *jihad* against "the faithless ones." He raised an army of fanatics and attacked Muslim rulers. His forces decimated a 10,000-man Egyptian army, besieged Khartoum, and slaughtered its defenders, including British General "Chinese" Gordon. The Mahdi died, and his successor continued the war. When the Egyptians called for more British help, Sir Herbert Kitchener arrived with young Winston Churchill among his officers. Their brigade used Britain's new Maxim guns to kill 20,000 Mahdists in one day. (A British quip at the time said foreign disputes would be resolved in Britain's favor "for we have got the Maxim gun and they have not.")

The British ruled Sudan for half a century, during which Christian missionaries converted much of the populace in the deep south. Britain agreed to leave in

1956, but the Christians and other southerners foresaw that Muslims from the north would attempt to impose Islam on them. They began rebelling in 1955. The warfare continued for seventeen years, killing an estimated 500,000 people. A truce finally was reached in 1972.

In 1983, a new Islamic president decreed the *shariá* for all of Sudan—and once again the southerners rebelled. The second war was worse than the first: hundreds of thousands of civilians died in the combat, and the disruption of agriculture caused famines that killed even greater numbers. Despite United Nations' food shipments, an estimated 250,000 southerners starved in 1988 alone.

Meanwhile, imposition of the *shariá* made the north a nightmare zone. In an eighteen-month period, 400 thieves had one or more hands axed with ceremonial swords. "Amputation days" were announced in newspapers, drawing crowds of the faithful who chanted "God is great" while swordsmen waved severed hands and feet. (Different Muslim societies seem to have different rules about when the *shariá* requires a hand or a foot to be chopped off. Reports in the 1980s told of both being amputated in Sudan's public ceremonies.) Floggings were inflicted for possessing alcohol. Morality patrols detained couples on the streets. Married pairs began carrying their wedding papers to prove legitimacy.

The barbarity caused international protest. One Sudanese Muslim leader, Mahmoud Taha, called for repeal of *shariá*. He was charged with heresy and hanged before a chanting crowd. Others kept silent lest they meet the same fate. Francis Deng of the Brookings Institution says it is difficult to undo the laws because backsliding in Islam is punishable by death. When the Muslim government relented in 1989 and promised to "freeze" the application of *shariá* in the south, fundamentalists overthrew the regime and vowed to enforce the Islamic code forever.

Extremists enacted a 1991 law requiring non-Muslims to memorize the Koran and attend Islamic schools. Women had to be cloaked. The new law also barred non-Muslims from government jobs and forbade them to testify against Muslims in court. And it decreed death for Muslims who rejected their faith.

Government publications began referring to Christians as "infidels" and instruments of "satanic" plots. *New Scientist* magazine (March 17, 1990) reported that a biology professor at the University of Khartoum was jailed and tortured because of allegations that he taught the theory of evolution. In late June of 1994, Amnesty International reported that in November of 1993, eight men caught drinking alcohol at a party in the city of Wad Medani were flogged with forty lashes each.

Condemnation of Sudan has come from many sources. Amnesty International said the Muslim forces are guilty of torture and wanton killings. The human rights group known as Middle East Concern said that the Muslim government utilized both famine and brutality to achieve "ethnic cleansing of the non-Muslim population." The United Nations appointed a human rights investigator for Sudan in 1993. Pope John Paul II, Jimmy Carter, and the Archbishop of Canterbury all visited the stricken land.

Rebuked by the international community, Sudan's

fundamentalist government formed an alliance with another pariah, the fanatical Muslim state of Iran, which promotes religious terrorism. Reports in 1993 stated that Iran was paying for camps in Sudan where Muslim radicals from Egypt, Algeria, and Tunisia were being trained in tactics to overthrow the secular governments of their nations.

Meanwhile, rival Muslim groups in Sudan fought each other. In 1994, the main mosque of the Ansar Sunna sect in Omdurman, across the Nile from Khartoum, was assaulted by opponents in a battle that took sixteen lives.

The U.S. State Department ruled in 1992 that Sudan is a terrorist state that "has pursued religiously extremist policies." U.N. envoy Gaspar Biro said in 1994 that *sharia*-style amputations, stonings, and floggings violate human rights. Sudan's military leader, Omar el-Bashir, replied that Biro is an "enemy of Islam" who wants "to erase the faith of Allah from the surface of the earth."

By mid-February of 1994, the Associated Press reported that the death toll of the second Sudanese civil war was estimated at 1.5 million, and about 6 million refugees had clogged surrounding regions. Rebel leader Riak Machar appealed for intervention by the United Nations. He said Muslim forces are bent on extinguishing "the entire south Sudanese civilian population through starvation [as well as] ethnic and religious cleansing. In certain parts of southern Sudan, human life has been completely wiped out."

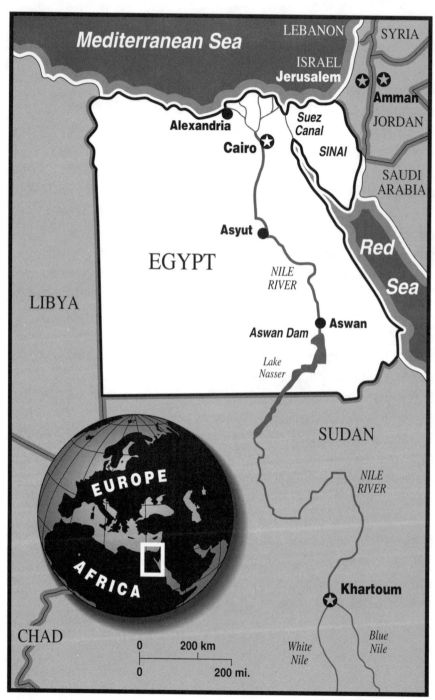

Bill Pitzer- PITZO*Graphics*

6

Egypt

Several Muslim nations that have evolved into secular states now fear the specter of Iran. They are suffering fundamentalist violence of the sort that overwhelmed Iran in 1979, transforming it into a cruel theocracy.

Egypt is a conspicuous victim of the trend. Muslim extremists who want to make Egypt a puritanical Islamic state commit terrorism almost daily, killing Coptic* Christian "infidels," burning nightclubs, and ambushing Western tourists to damage the image of the secular government. Brutal police counterattacks and executions haven't stamped out the movement.

Egypt's agony began in 1980, just after the militant

---

*An indigenous Egyptian group, which split from other Christians in the fifth century in a quarrel over whether Jesus was "god-man" or "god and man."

takeover in Iran. Fundamentalists in Egypt's *Al Jihad* group planted bombs in Coptic Christian churches and killed families at Coptic weddings. Others in the Muslim Brotherhood denounced President Anwar Sadat as a religious traitor because he had signed a peace treaty with Israel.

The spiritual leader of the zealots was a blind holy man named Sheik Omar Abdel Rahman, who ranted against secularism. He told the faithful that death was the proper punishment of a Muslim ruler who betrayed Allah. When militants wanted to rob a Christian jewelry store to get money for guns, they asked Rahman for a *fatwa*, a religious edict, declaring that robbery for a holy purpose wasn't sinful.

As ferment grew in Egypt in 1981, Sadat cracked down. The police seized 1,600 activists, banned fifteen Muslim extremist groups, halted radical Muslim publications, exiled the Coptic pope, and imprisoned the head of the Muslim Brotherhood. But it was too late: on October 6, 1981, while Sadat reviewed a military parade in the Nasser City suburb east of Cairo, fanatics in an army unit leaped out of the ranks and assassinated him in a hail of bullets. The killers boasted that they did it for Allah.

Twenty-four conspirators were arrested, including Sheik Rahman. The indictment alleged that the fundamentalists had planned to install him as Egypt's ayatollah in a holy government. He was accused of telling the plotters that Sadat and other leaders were atheists who deserved to die. News reports said police found $20,000 hidden in Rahman's underwear. In the subsequent trial, twenty-two people were convicted and five were hanged, but Sheik Rahman and another person were acquitted.

Religious rebellion became a constant threat in Egypt, with its recurring violence. Two days after Anwar Sadat's murder, fundamentalists stormed a police station at Asyut, and eighty-seven died in a battle with troops. Waves of arrests failed to eliminate the danger.

The new government of President Hosni Mubarak attempted to appease the zealots. Egypt's parliament voted in 1985 to restudy the country's laws, to make them conform with the *shariá*. The courts also banned *Arabian Nights* because holy men had labeled it obscene, and licenses for belly dancers were restricted. The government also banned religious bumper stickers on cars because Muslims and Copts clashed over them.

The Muslim Brotherhood renounced violence—publicly, at least—and the *Jihad* group went underground, but random bloodshed continued. In 1986, fundamentalist youths assaulted and burned a dozen nightclubs near the pyramids. Two former cabinet ministers were wounded by terrorists in 1987. The same year, Muslims attacked Copts because of a rumor that a secret Coptic spray caused Christian crosses to appear on Muslim women's veils. On college campuses, fundamentalist students attacked secular students participating in coed activities. Rioting in 1989 caused the arrest of 1,500 Muslim zealots, including Sheik Rahman.

Rahman called for the assassination of Nobel Prize-winning writer Naguib Mahfouz on grounds that one of his early books, *The Children of Gebelawi*, "insulted Islam." Mahfouz, then 78, replied whimsically: "At my age, any killing must be considered a natural death." The book remains banned in Egypt, more than thirty years after it was published.

The agitation for an Islamic theocracy intensified: riots against Copts in 1990 occurred in five cities, and assassins killed the speaker of Egypt's parliament and five others on a Cairo street. Terrorists also killed eight Israeli tourists on an Egyptian bus. In 1992, they murdered writer Faraq Fouda, who had sneered at fundamentalism. When Fouda's killers were brought to trial, holy man Mohammed al-Ghazali testified in their defense, saying that a secularist "must be eliminated. It is the duty of the government to kill him."

To extend Mahfouz's sarcasm, murder may be a natural death for any skeptical writer among fundamentalists. Many of Egypt's intellectuals are at risk. For example, the *Washington Post* reported on July 22, 1993, that Nasr Abu Zeid, an assistant professor of Arabic at Cairo University, was denied promotion to full professor because a colleague complained that his research contained "talk similar to atheism." Then fundamentalists denounced Abu Zeid as an apostate who has rejected his faith. Next, a fundamentalist lawyer filed court proceedings to force Abu Zeid and his wife to divorce, because an apostate cannot be married to a Muslim. When a judge refused to dismiss the proceedings, the Egyptian Organization of Human Rights protested that the court action against Abu Zeid "in the prevailing atmosphere of religious intoler-

Hospital staff carry out victims gunned down by Muslim militants seeking revenge for the death of their leader. (Reuters/Bettmann)

ance . . . exposes him and his wife to the danger of assassination by some political Islamic group that believes it is their duty to murder apostates." The Abu Zeids received death threats. The teacher said that calling a person an apostate is "legalizing his murder," so he and his wife prepared to leave Egypt.

Copts suffered worse attacks. Thirteen were massacred in 1992 at the village of Sanabu, just northwest of Asyut. Guards outside Coptic cathedrals and churches were gunned down. Two Copts died when young Muslim militants burned the Christian church at Biba, a town of 50,000 on the west bank of the Nile, south of Cairo. A fundamentalist screaming "God is great!" stabbed a Coptic student to death at Asyut. Terrorists repeatedly robbed Copt-owned jewelry and liquor stores to fund their movement and also to smite the infidels for their alcohol and coquetry. Many Coptic homes and stores were burned. In February 1994, a Muslim police commander gunned down two Christian fellow officers. The following month, drive-by terrorists killed a boy, two priests, and two passersby standing outside a Coptic monastery in Asyut. The same month, a Coptic hairdresser was stabbed to death at Asyut, presumably by fanatics who deem it sinful for a man to touch a woman who is not his wife.

Fundamentalist attacks on belly-dancing escalated. "This is adulterous filth," hard-line parliament member Maamoun Hodeibi declared. Religious leader Mahmoud Khodari vowed that his followers would flog the dancers for violating the taboo forbidding a woman to show herself to anyone except her husband. An Islamic weekly newspaper declared: "Belly-dancing epitomizes the sickness of man's soul. By crushing it, we take the first leap toward godliness." In such an attempt molotov cocktails were thrown into clubs where belly-dancers worked.

Systematic ambushes of police and security commanders began in 1992. So did attacks on tourists. Visitors to the pyramids and the tombs at Luxor, at a bulge of the Nile midway between Aswan and Asyut, faced constant peril from snipers or bombers. Egypt's lucrative tourist trade plummeted. The following are a sampling of incidents that have occurred:

Machine gunners sprayed the motorcade of General Osman Shaheen, killing two people. Two of the assassins died in return fire.

*   *   *

A fanatic screaming "God is great!" opened fire in a Cairo luxury hotel, killing American and French tourists.

*   *   *

Interior Minister Hassan al-Alfi was wounded by a bomb that killed four.

*   *   *

The outlawed Islamic Group bombed an American bank in Cairo in 1994, warning Muslims to withdraw their money from banks that violate Islam's prohibition on interest.

*   *   *

Fanatics killed three vacationers on a tour bus near Asyut, stabbed three Russian tourists at Port Said at the northern end of the Suez Canal, and fired at a cruise ship carrying German tourists on the Nile River.

*   *   *

Terrorists tossed two bombs at a tourist bus carrying Austrian Christians to visit the Coptic Hanging Church, a spot supposedly visited by the holy family on their flight into Egypt. One bomb injured eight Austrians. The other bounced off the bus and injured eight Muslims on a sidewalk.

*   *   *

Police engaged terrorists around Asyut in an all-night gun battle that killed eight fundamentalists and five officers.

*   *   *

When Prime Minister Atef Sedki visited a grade school, a car bomb exploded outside and killed an eleven-year-old girl. In connection with the attack, fifteen fundamentalists were charged. Nine of them were sentenced to death

88

A defendant holds the Koran and chants during a trial of Muslim militants charged with attacking tourists. (Reuters/Bettmann)

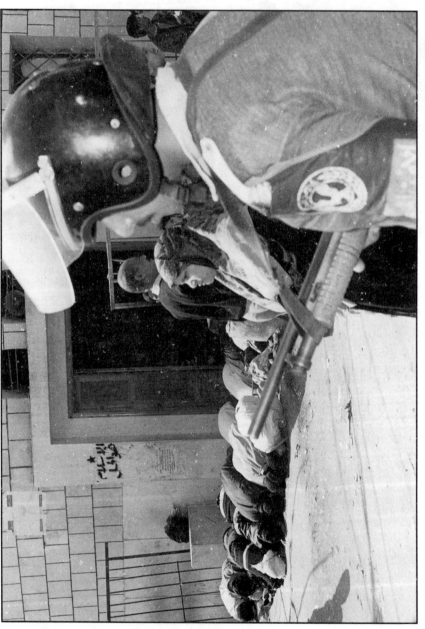

Egyptian troops stand guard as Muslims perform Friday noon prayers at the Imbaba Mosque. Security forces killed 16 Muslim militants in raids at Imbaba and elsewhere. (Reuters/Bettmann)

in 1994. They fell to the courtroom floor in prayer, shouting "We are going to heaven." As they were led to a police van, one chanted: "The Islamic state is coming."

Desperately striving to end the ferment, President Mubarak's government tried both appeasement and Gestapo tactics. To mollify the fanatics, the sale of alcohol was banned in fourteen of Egypt's twenty-six districts, books criticizing fundamentalism were confiscated at Cairo's International Book Fair, and author Alaa Hamid was sentenced to prison for "blasphemy" because one of his books questioned the validity of all religions. American evangelists were arrested on charges of trying to convert Muslims to Christianity. Egyptian television began broadcasting more religious shows, and national leaders made the *hajj*, the holy pilgrimage to Mecca, with TV crews along. All that was the inducement side of the carrot-and-stick approach. The cudgel was commando-like police raids. In December 1992, President Mubarak sent 14,000 officers and one hundred armored vehicles on a sweep through Imbaba, one of Cairo's fundamentalist neighborhoods. Hundreds were arrested. In March 1993, officers stormed a mosque at Aswan in a firefight that killed 14; more died in raids around Cairo. Military courts condemned scores of accused terrorists. The government hanged 39 in 1993, even though judges freed 24 others after deciding that "the ugliest forms of torture" had been inflicted on them.

Neither force nor concessions slowed the attacks. By 1994, about 350 people had died in the two years of terrorism. Middle East scholar Dr. Alon Ben-Meir says the zealots eventually may win and turn Egypt into another Iran. Fundamentalism is drawing millions of followers from Egypt's dismal slums, he says. With poverty rampant and few jobs available, those at the bottom see little hope except in the promises of religion. A March 1993 *Newsweek* story states that walls in Muslim quarters are scrawled with slogans such as "God curses the Christians and Jews." The most resentful believers are recruited by the clandestine murder groups. Thus the blight of poverty produces the blight of religious terrorism.

Egypt's chief judge, Muhammed Ashmawy, declared that fundamentalist Islam is basically "totalitarian." The government erected billboards showing crazed terrorists, with the message: "They do not belong to Islam." Under the guise of "protecting houses of worship," officials began taking control of mosques to halt insurrectionist preaching.

President Mubarak denounces the "plague" of extremism, and also belittles it. The fundamentalists, he says, want to "gag mouths, suppress opinion, and sequester freedom." As for Sheik Rahman, the president said: "He thinks he is another Ayatollah Khomeini, but there is a great difference between them: the followers of this so-called sheik are less than a tenth of one percent of Egyptians."

For so tiny a group, they have inflicted terrible harm on their nation.

On a map Egypt appears vast, but actually it's a thin snake of a country. Virtually all the population is concentrated in the Nile Valley, while the rest of the county is desert. In the 1990s, murder plots by furtive fundamentalists are a serpent within this serpentine society.

A bomb placed behind a stone column in a packed Cairo coffee shop exploded killing two tourists and injuring 18 others. (AP/Wide World Photos)

The twin towers of the World Trade Center, in which a terrorist bomb killed five and injured hundreds. (AP/Wide World Photos)

7

The New York City Plot

Holy hatred in Egypt begat holy terror in New York City. After Sheik Omar Abdel Rahman was arrested three times for preaching the murder of those in Egypt who he believed violated strict Islamic law, he turned his attention to the international scene. In the late 1980s, he took two of his sons to Pakistan, where they joined the CIA-backed Muslim warriors fighting to free Afghanistan from communism (and make it a theocracy). The blind holy man praised the Afghan war as a *jihad* against infidels. Rahman's various wives remained in Egypt.*

Rahman eventually went to Sudan in 1990, visited the U.S. Embassy, and obtained a visa to enter the country.

---

*As reported in *Newsweek*, March 29, 1993, p. 38, and *Time*, October 4, 1993, p. 60.

His name was on a State Department "watch list" of suspected terrorists, so the visa shouldn't have been granted. Some U.S. officials blamed a Sudanese civilian employee of the embassy, but *Time* magazine reported that the visa was granted by a CIA agent in Khartoum.* Egyptian President Hosni Mubarak later charged: "The sheik has been a CIA agent since his days in Afghanistan. The visa he got was not issued by mistake. It was because of the services he did."† Officials in Washington denied it.

After arriving in the United States, Rahman began his radical tirades at a Jersey City mosque. (U.S. authorities think Rahman lived on money from Iran funneled through one of his wives in Egypt.‡) A clique of Muslim fanatics grew around the charismatic preacher. Cassette tapes of his fiery sermons were sent back for circulation among his followers in Egypt. He brazenly urged the overthrow of the "satanic" Mubarak government. One tape exhorted believers: "Hit hard and kill the enemies of God in every spot, to rid it of the descendants of apes and pigs fed at the tables of Zionism, communism, and imperialism. There is no truce in *jihad* against the enemies of Allah."**

A circle of Muslim immigrant worshipers in the New Jersey mosque plotted terrorism. The first murder happened in late 1990. The target was Rabbi Meir Kahane of New York, a Jewish extremist who was somewhat a mirror image of Sheik Rahman. Born in Brooklyn, Kahane

---

*See *Time,* July 19, 1993, p. 42.
†Ibid.
‡*Newsweek,* March 232, 1993, p. 33.
**Newsweek,* March 15, 1993, p. 32.

founded the armed Jewish Defense League that used force against anti-Semitism. He immigrated to Israel in 1971, and there he founded the Arab-hating Kach party that advocated "ethnic cleansing" of Muslims. He demanded that the 2.5 million Palestinians in Israel, the Gaza Strip, and the West Bank be expelled, as Jews once were from Christian nations of Europe. Kahane served four years in Israel's parliament (the Knesset), but he and his extremist party finally were banished. He soon returned to New York, where he was a hero to Jewish militants.

Kahane was giving a speech at a Manhattan hotel on November 5, 1990, when he was shot to death by a man in the audience. One of Sheik Rahman's disciples, El Sayyid Nosair, ran from the room and was captured after a gunfight with a postal officer. Kahane's New York followers screamed "Death to Arabs" and vowed retaliation. Rabbi Kahane's body was returned to Jerusalem for burial. During the funeral procession, Kach adherents smashed Muslim shops and chased Muslims along the streets.

In a 1991 New York trial, witnesses couldn't identify Nosair as the killer in the hotel ballroom, but he was convicted as the running gunman who wounded the postal officer and a bystander. He was sentenced to a prison term.

This much publicized political/religious assassination was then followed by the horrendous 1993 explosion in the World Trade Center that killed six, injured 1,000, and caused extensive damage. America was visibly shaken. Several of Sheik Rahman's proteges had rented a van, packed it with homemade fuel-and-fertilizer explosive, and

Workers sift through the rubble beneath the World Trade Center in search of victims and survivors. (AP/Wide World Photos)

parked it in the Trade Center garage. The amateur terrorists were caught quickly by police.

An hour after the New York blast, an explosion shattered a Cairo cafe, killing four people and injuring eighteen. The victims included Egyptians and tourists.

Six months later, U.S. prosecutors obtained a massive indictment against Sheik Rahman and fourteen followers, accusing them of waging holy war in America. In addition to the Kahane murder and the Trade Center bombing, it charged them with plotting to blow up the United Nations, two New York tunnels and a Justice Department building. The indictment stated that Rahman sought to hire an assassin to kill Egyptian President Hosni Mubarak.

After the case broke, news reports portrayed the defendants as obsessive fundamentalists, consumed by their defensive dedication to Islam. They bow to Mecca five times a day in prostrate prayer. Several of them had been affiliated with a Brooklyn Muslim center that recruited volunteer holy warriors to go to Afghanistan. (According to a *Newsweek* story dated March 29, 1993, the director of the center was found murdered after quarreling with Sheik Rahman.) Ironically, some of the World Trade Center bombers had gone to Afghanistan, where they were taught terror tactics by the CIA during the Cold War against the former Soviet Union.

When Rahman was jailed by U.S. authorities, the Associated Press reported in March of 1993 that his followers in Egypt vowed to "take revenge on all U.S. interests and citizens, either in Egypt or outside, if any harm comes to Sheik Omar."

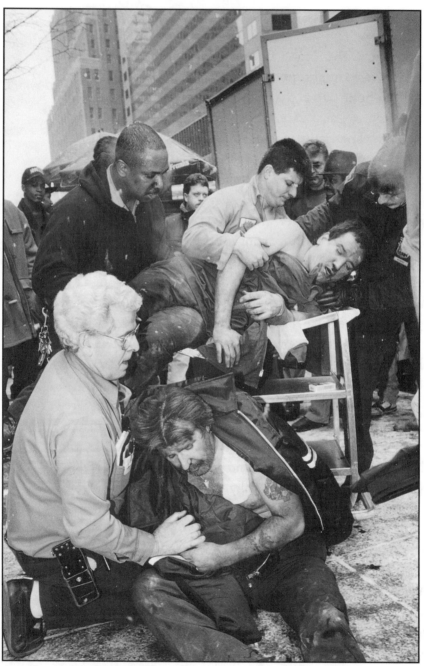

Survivors of the World Trade Center bombing are aided by rescue personnel. (AP/Wide World Photos)

Strong statements weren't limited to Muslim militants. *Time* magazine reported in September of 1993 that the sheik's defense lawyer, Ron Kuby, said federal prosecutors were "using the criminal justice system to indict a religious group for religious teaching." Referring to American Catholics who attack abortion clinics, he compared Sheik Rahman to Pope John Paul II. "Why wasn't the pope taken into custody when he visited Denver?" Kuby asked. "He is the spiritual leader of abortion clinic bombers and doctor killers."

Four of the defendants were prosecuted in a six-month trial. All four were found guilty in 1994. As the verdict was read, they raged, pounded courtroom tables, and shouted in Arabic: "God is great! . . . Victory to Islam!"

After the trial, transcripts of FBI surveillance tapes showed that the plotters had talked about kidnapping Henry Kissinger and holding him hostage for release of Muslim prisoners. They also considered sniper attacks on Jewish leaders in Manhattan, and called the United Nations "the house of the devil." Defense lawyer William Kunstler shrugged off the tapes, saying, "These guys are hopped-up guys, Islamic fundamentalists. They have wild thoughts, no questions about it. But wild thoughts are not a crime."

The convicted bombers staged a hunger strike in their cells. Later, all four were sentenced to 240-year prison terms.

In mid-1994, while Sheik Rahman was being held in a U.S. prison awaiting trial for the New York City bombing and for the murder of Rabbi Kahane, an Egyptian court convicted him *in absentia* of terrorism and sentenced him to seven years at hard labor. Professor Amos Perlmutter of American University said the terrorists chose the World Trade Center because it signifies American luxury. "The target was symbolic, an example of everything fundamentalists see as evil in the West." He added, ominously: "The bombing was only the first in a fundamentalist assault on America."*

Terrorism experts Nathan Adams and Yossef Bodansky warned that Sheik Rahman's clique isn't the only Muslim fanatic group in America. Similar cells are getting furtive support from Iran to attack "the Great Satan," they said. Adams said one tactic recommended by Iran was "poisoning a large city's water supply with a deadly biological warfare agent."†

In his 1993 book, *Target America*, Bodansky, director of Congress' House Republican Task Force on Terrorism, predicted that the World Trade Tower attack was "but a prelude to an escalation of Islamist terrorism in the United States and Canada." He said Muslims from all nations who fought in Afghanistan are now known throughout the Muslim world as "Afghans." They have joined violent groups such as *Hezbollah* and the Armed Islamic Movement (AIM), Bodansky wrote, and are making their way into cliques in America. He said: "The Islamist terrorists *know* that their objective will ultimately be realized through Allah's will. The belief in this inevitability can be compared to the belief in miracles. . . . The terrorists of *Hezbollah*‡ and AIM are motivated by rage

---

*Scholastic Update, October 22, 1993, p. 11.
†*Target America: Terrorism in the U.S. Today* (New York: S.P.I. Books, 1993).
‡Italics added.

and the desire for revenge. . . . In the wake of the Gulf War, Arabs feel shamed and humiliated. . . . Iranian warnings throughout the 1980s of U.S. hostility toward Arabs and Muslims were 'confirmed' in the Gulf War by the fury of the air campaign and the magnitude of the damage. Consequently, a growing number of volunteers join the ranks of those who are eager and ready to kill and die for the Islamists' cause."

Another Muslim group waging holy war in America was reported in the February 28, 1994, issue of *Newsweek* magazine. It said *Al-Fuqra* (The Impoverished), founded by Pakistani sheik Mubarak Shah Jilani, "is now considered perhaps the most dangerous fundamentalist sect operating in the United States." While the World Trade Center bombers attained notoriety, the magazine said, *Al-Fuqra's* 3,000 mostly black members "have perpetrated far more havoc. Law enforcement officials say they are responsible for a decade-long string of assassinations and bombings in the name of Islamic purity."

The report said *Al-Fuqra*, based in a Brooklyn mosque, attacks other religious believers, including Hindus, Hare Krishnas, Jews, and even rival Black Muslims. These incidents were cited:

An Oregon hotel owned by Bhagwan Sri Rajneesh, the late Indian guru, was firebombed in 1983. An *Al-Fuqra* leader, Stephen Paster, blew off part of his hand while preparing explosives for the assault. He served four years in prison.

* * *

The same year, a leader of a Detroit Muslim sect was shot to death. *Al-Fuqra* members suspected of the assassination died in a firebombing of their headquarters.

* * *

Hare Krishna temples in Philadelphia and Denver were firebombed in 1984.

* * *

In 1993, *Al-Fuqra* member James Williams was convicted in the murder of an Arizona *imam*, Rashid Khalifa, who preached that the Koran was written by man, not Allah.

* * *

Also in 1993, three suspected members were convicted of conspiring to blow up a Hindu temple and an Indian theater in Toronto, Canada.

* * *

Newsweek noted that an *Al-Fuqra* member was among the defendants charged in Sheik Rahman's plot to blow up the United Nations and other New York City sites.

* * *

Another Muslim plot in America had a grotesque outcome. FBI agents suspected that Palestinian immigrant Zian Isa and three colleagues were planning terrorism, so they secretly planted listening devices in Isa's apartment in St. Louis. As the federal agents were listening on November 6, 1989, they were horrified to hear Isa and his wife stab their sixteen-year-old daughter to death because she had adopted irreligious American habits. The girl's screams and the parents' angry accusations were recorded on a seven-minute tape. The father shouted in Arabic, "Die quickly, my daughter, die," as he stabbed her six times in the chest. Both parents were convicted of murder in 1991 and sentenced to death. The wife's sentence was later reduced on appeal.

In 1993, Isa and his three Palestinian associates were indicted on terrorism conspiracy charges. The three colleagues pleaded guilty in July, 1994. U.S. attorneys decided not to prosecute Isa further, on grounds that he was ill and awaiting execution for his daughter's murder.

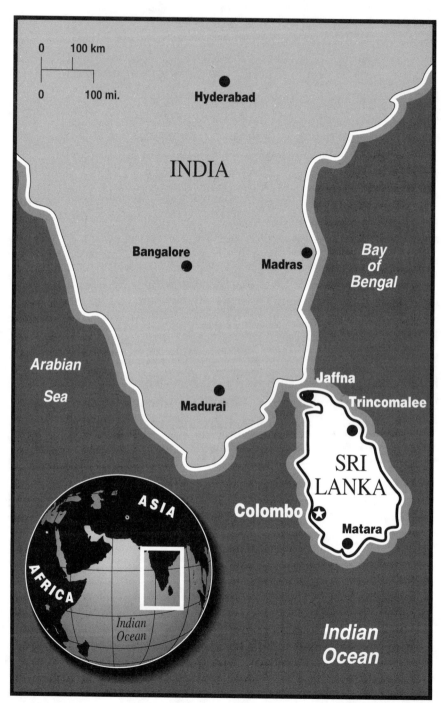

Bill Pitzer- PITZOGraphics

8

Sri Lanka

Three Gandhis of India were felled by religious tribalism. Mohandas Gandhi, the great "Mahatma" who shamed the British into freeing their colony, was murdered in 1948 by a Hindu fanatic during the Muslim-Hindu horror that followed the British pullout. Nearly forty years later, Prime Minister Indira Gandhi* was murdered in 1984 by Sikh zealots among her guards. And seven years thereafter, Prime Minister Rajiv Gandhi, son of Indira, was murdered by agents of Hindu Tamils embroiled in a ghastly civil war with Buddhist Sinhalese in Sri Lanka.

Sri Lanka, the island formerly called Ceylon, hangs like a teardrop below India's southern tip. A teardrop might

---

*No relation to the Mahatma; she was a daughter of leader Jawaharlal Nehru and married a Gandhi.

well be its national symbol because 20,000 of the island's people have been killed in the decade-long conflict rooted in social, political, religious, and ethnic hostilities.

The trouble began more than a millennium ago when Tamils from India invaded and drove the Sinhalese natives southward. Ever since, three-fourths of the population has been southern Buddhists, while one-fifth is Hindus in the northeast. The rest are Muslims and Christians. Violent clashes between Buddhists and Muslims occurred in the 1800s. In the twentieth century the hate has been between Buddhists and Hindus.

The British freed Ceylon in 1948 after leaving India. A Buddhist-dominated government was established. Buddhist festivals became national holidays. Much of public life centered on pilgrimages to the Temple of the Tooth, which supposedly contains one of Buddha's teeth, and to a rock supposedly containing Buddha's footprint. (The rock is on a mountain that became the home of Adam and Eve after they were driven out of the Garden of Eden, according to Sri Lanka's Muslims.)

Hindus largely were left out of Sri Lanka's society. In the late 1950s, a Buddhist prime minister increased the Buddhist supremacy by declaring Sinhalese to be the only official language. When Hindus protested, he vacillated, and was soon assassinated by a Buddhist monk who considered him a traitor to the faith.

Since that time the outnumbered Hindus have chafed at discrimination by the Buddhist majority. Militants among them demanded a separate nation in the northeast. In 1983, a budding Hindu guerrilla movement ambushed an army patrol. Buddhists were enraged, and retaliated by massacring hundreds of Hindus across Sri Lanka. In retaliation, armed Hindu bands swept into Buddhist holy spots, killing as many as 173 in a single raid.

Full civil war erupted. Five different Hindu rebel groups—especially a fanatical army called the Liberation Tigers—waged hit-and-run attacks. Massacres, ambushes, bombings, executions, and other horrors have continued for more than a decade. Nearly 200,000 Hindus fled the island as refugees. As the slaughter progressed, much of the impetus came from a desire by each side to avenge atrocities committed by the other.

Guerrillas lined up Buddhist monks and shot them down. Government troops retaliated by lining up Hindu villagers for counterexecutions. Hindu brigades suspected that Muslims were backing the government, so they invaded Muslim mosques and killed worshipers.

Hindus in southern India, separated by only a fifty-mile-wide strait, aided the Hindu rebels. At first, the Hindu government of India sent supplies. But Prime Minister Rajiv Gandhi switched to neutrality. In 1987, he sent a 70,000-man peacekeeping force to separate the warring groups. But combat broke out between the rebels and the Indian soldiers. The "peacekeeping force" lost 1,000 men before being withdrawn in 1990.

A headstrong Tiger leader vowed revenge on Prime Minister Gandhi. He gained it in 1991 by sending a young Tiger woman girdled with explosives as a human bomb. As Gandhi arrived for an election rally at a southern Indian

Young Hindu Tamil Tiger "Cubs" in the Sri Lankan jungle await their next opportunity to strike at Buddhist government forces. (AP/Wide World Photos)

town, she detonated the charge, killing herself, the prime minister and sixteen others.

Police rounded up other Tigers suspected of being backup members of the assassination team. As officers closed in, a Tiger leader killed himself with a pistol and six others took their lives by biting cyanide capsules. The remaining suspects finally were put on trial in 1994.

Meanwhile, the murder rate snowballed in Sri Lanka, especially in its capital of Colombo. In 1991, a Hindu car bomb killed the deputy defense minister and twenty-nine others. In 1992, a suicide bomber on a motorcycle killed Sri Lanka's naval commander. In 1993, another Hindu suicide bomber killed President Ranasinghe Premadasa and a dozen others at a May Day parade.

In 1994, decapitation was added to the nightmare. Buddhist police beheaded one of several rebels who attacked a station, and Hindu terrorists retaliated by killing police and then chopping off their heads.

The decade of religio-ethnic horror has devastated the lovely island. Thousands have died, the damage toll has been vast, and military costs have devoured much of Sri Lanka's wealth. This tropical paradise has become a hell on earth.

Villagers watch a burning corpse dumped along a road. Burning bodies are found almost every morning in southern and central Sri Lanka as Buddhist extremists fight with government forces. (AP/Wide World Photos)

Iran

Bill Pitzer- PITZOGraphics

9

Iran

The world's most religious government also is the cruelest. Iran's Shi'ite theocracy, which calls itself "the government of God on earth," remained as vicious in the 1990s as it was in the 1980s. After the 1989 death of the fundamentalist state's cold-eyed founder, the Ayatollah Khomeini, international hope rose that Iran might become more humane. It was a false hope. Instead, these developments occurred:

The ayatollah's *fatwa* (holy edict) calling for murder of "blaspheming" author Salman Rushdie was reaffirmed overwhelmingly by Iran's parliament in 1993. An Iranian "religious charity," the Khordad 15 Foundation, raised its bounty offer on Rushdie's head to $3 million.

* * *

Three leaders of the minority Baha'i faith were sentenced to death as "unprotected infidels" in 1993, raising fear of a resumption of the executions that killed 200 Baha'is in the early 1980s and caused 40,000 to flee the country.

*　*　*

Iran sent assassin teams abroad to kill a dozen secularists and dissidents around Europe. It also supported fundamentalist terrorism in Egypt, Algeria, Jordan, and elsewhere. The U.S. State Department branded Iran in 1993 as "the world's most dangerous state sponsor of terrorism."

*　*　*

Iran's parliament drafted a law in 1994 to execute repeat sellers of sexual movies or magazines.

*　*　*

Amnesty International, the worldwide human rights monitor, reported in 1993 that Iran employs the death penalty more than any other nation, that it tortures suspects, and that it tramples the rights of women.

*　*　*

In 1994, a United Nations human rights report reiterated the charges and condemned Iran's many executions. A reply by the Iranian government said the death penalty is "rooted in divine principles."

*   *   *

Under Iran's puritanical dress code, women must be covered from head to toe, except for their faces. No lock of hair may be seen. No makeup or nail polish may be worn. Morality police called *komitehs* patrol the streets to look for offenders. Amnesty International said hundreds of women were arrested in a 1993 crackdown and sentenced to floggings of seventy-two lashes each. The human rights group called the floggings "cruel, inhuman, and degrading punishment, forbidden under international law." Other reports said many Iranian women were stoned to death for adultery.

Iran, formerly Persia, has a deep heritage of religious violence. Its people are mostly Shi'ites, a rebellious group that evolved in Islam's gory infancy. After the Prophet Muhammad spread the faith by *jihad*, he died unexpectedly in 632, and one of his aged fathers-in-law was named his successor, or *caliph*. The old man lived only two years. He was succeeded by another father-in-law, Umar, who escalated the holy wars, conquering a vast empire for Islam. Umar was murdered, and one of Muhammad's sons-in-law, Uthman, was named the third *caliph*. A different son-in-law, Ali, was rejected.

When Uthman also was murdered, Ali was rejected a second time, causing his supporters, now called Shi'ites, to rebel against the majority Muslims. Then Ali was assassinated by a fanatic, and the Shi'ites rallied around his son Husayn. But the son was killed in a battle with the dominant Muslims (an event many Shi'ites still observe by whipping themselves bloody on the anniversary of the battle).

Ever since the death of Ali, Shi'ites have been a resentful minority, periodically waging *jihads* against majority Sunnis. Iran became a Shi'ite land in the early 1500s when a ruler decreed that Shi'ah was the only allowable faith.

The word *shi'ah* derives from *shi'at Ali* (partisans of Ali). Theologically, there's little difference between Shi'ah and Sunnah Islam. Believers of each branch worship a lone Allah. Both sides revere the Prophet Muhammad and hold sacred the Koran, which he dictated. All the faithful bow five times daily toward Mecca. All dream of a heavenly paradise full of lovely Houri nymphs. Differences center chiefly around the line of succession from the prophet.

In the mid-1800s, some Iranians began following a holy man who said he was "The Gate" through whom a long-vanished prophet spoke. Shi'ite leaders sent The Gate to a firing squad, massacred many of his followers, and imprisoned others. One of the prisoners, Baha'ullah, declared himself to be the messiah of every religion—thus the Baha'i faith was born. It gathered thousands of believers throughout Iran. Shi'ite mullahs denounced Baha'is as heretics. Bloody persecutions have been waged upon them for a century. For example, in 1955, a fierce *mullah*, preaching by radio, called for Iranians to smite the "false religion." A wave of murder, rape, arson, and destruction followed, ending only when the United Nations intervened.

Fanaticism attained its golden age in Iran in 1979, when

supporters of the exiled Ayatollah Khomeini overthrew the government of the Shah and installed a fundamentalist theocracy. In addition to holding fifty-two hostages from the U.S. Embassy in Teheran in miserable captivity for 444 days, the religious regime sickened the world with a horrifying wave of executions, floggings, torture, stonings, and jailings.

Baha'is were the chief victims. A top religious judge, Jujjatu'l-Islam Qazai, president of the revolutionary court of Shiraz, decreed that the new "government of God on earth" would not "tolerate the perverted Baha'is, who are instruments of Satan and followers of the devil."* Baha'is were denied jobs, education, pensions, and sometimes even homes. Many who refused to convert were executed. A Shi'ite judge justified the killings by quoting a Koran prayer: "Lord, leave not a single family of infidels on the earth." The U.S. Congress condemned Iran's "relentless acts of savagery against the innocent Baha'is."†

Khomeini raged against "the Great Satan," America. A street in the Iranian capital of Teheran was named Ahmad Ghasir Avenue in honor of the suicide bomber who drove a truckload of explosives into the U.S. Marine barracks at Beirut Airport in 1983, killing 241 Americans.

Then Khomeini plunged into combat with neighboring Iraq, calling the conflict a "war against blasphemy." The war began when Iraq's Saddam Hussein invaded a

---

*The Christian Century, December 3, 1986, p. 1095.

†House Concurrent Resolution 226, passed by Congress June 15, 1984, stated that "more than 150 members of the Baha'i faith have been brutally executed," while many others were "tortured, persecuted, and deprived of their fundamental rights." The resolution condemned the attempt by Iran's leaders "to destroy the Baha'i faith."

corner of Iran, and Khomeini sent human waves of young zealots to be mowed down in battle. He roused the fervor of soldiers, saying that "to kill the unbelievers is one of man's greatest missions." Khomeini usually spoke in hate-filled religious hyperbole, whatever the topic.

Khomeini also triggered riots in several Muslim nations in 1989 by demanding the execution of British author Salman Rushdie because his book *The Satanic Verses* implies in a dream sequence that Muhammad was a fraud. Rushdie has been in hiding ever since, a victim of what he calls the "heartless certainties" of rigid religious belief. The Japanese translator of his book was stabbed to death. Its Italian translator survived a 1991 stabbing. And in 1993, its Norwegian publisher was shot three times, but lived. Viking Penguin, the original publisher of *The Satanic Verses*, has been forced to spend $3 million a year for round-the-clock guards for editors in New York and London.

Muslims in London carried "Rushdie Must Die" signs. The British Muslim Action Front attempted to sue Rushdie and his publishers under Britain's blasphemy law, but a magistrate ruled that the law applies only to Christianity.

Every February, Iran celebrates "the day of God," the anniversary of the 1979 seizure of power. On that holy day in 1994, Iranian radio reported that "millions" of Shi'ites flooded the streets of Teheran, many of them screaming "Death to America."

On another holy day, known as *Ashura*, the anniversary of the seventh-century martyrdom of Husayn, hundreds of worshipers were praying in a saint's mausoleum at Mashhad when a bomb blast killed 26 and wounded

70. The government blamed rebels of the *Mujahideen Khalq* (People's Holy Warriors), but exiled leaders of the group denied involvement. Other reports blamed Iran's minority Sunnis, who feel persecuted in the Shi'ite nation. A few months earlier, Sunnis had rioted in Zahedan on the eastern border near the three-nation corner with Afghanistan and Pakistan, because of false rumors that Shi'ite authorities demolished a Sunni mosque.

Also in 1994, an Iranian Pentecostal leader, Haik Hovsepian-Mehr, who refused to obey a new law prohibiting attempts to convert Muslims, mysteriously was stabbed to death. After his family reported him missing, his body was found buried in a Muslim cemetery.

Not long thereafter, another talking-in-tongues minister, Mehdi Debaj, likewise was found murdered. Debaj, formerly a Muslim, had been imprisoned ten years, then he was sentenced to death for apostasy. But an international effort forced authorities to release him not long before he was killed. A *New York Times* analysis said Iran intensified its suppression of Christians in 1994, killing at least three Pentecostal leaders, jailing and torturing converts, and closing several churches.

Iran's 1979 capture by zealots introduced a new menace—"fundamentalist takeover." During the Cold War, "communist takeover" was the great dread: the fear that armed Reds would seize a nation and bring totalitarianism. Iran showed that armed zealots and holy men can be more totalitarian than even communists.

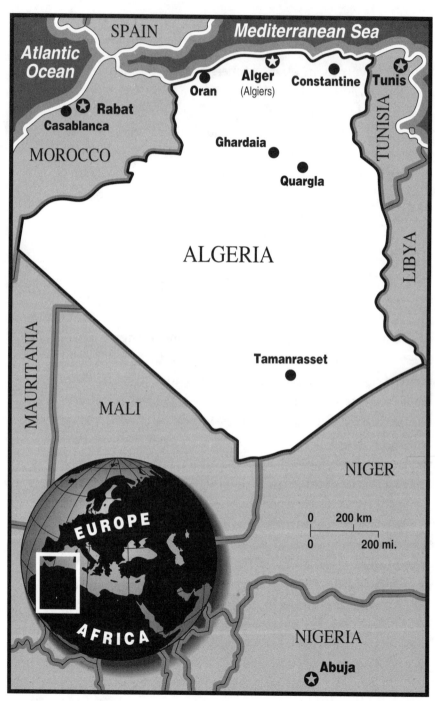

Bill Pitzer- PITZO*Graphics*

10

Algeria

The next violent fundamentalist takeover is likely to be in Algeria. By the time this book comes off the press, the sunny North African nation may have been seized by fanatics, and sheiks may be decreeing harsh punishments under the *shariá* religious law.

Algeria, a lovely part of the Mediterranean coast, was colonized nearly 3,000 years ago by seafaring Phoenicians. They built temples in which they sacrificed children to gods such as Astarte, Adonis, and Moloch. In the seventh century, Muslims waging holy war defeated Algerians led by the priestess Kahina. The land has been Muslim ever since. During the century when Algeria was a French colony, full French citizenship was offered to Algerians who renounced Islam. Few did, and a brutal rebellion finally drove out the French.

Algeria has been relatively modern and Westernized. After France freed the colony in 1962, at the end of a gory seven-year war, a socialist military government took power and operated a somewhat benign police state, with one-party elections. Life was sophisticated, with bikini-clad bathers on the Mediterranean beaches and cocktails in its nightclubs.

But the economy slumped, joblessness grew to 30 percent, and consumer goods and housing became scarce. Hard times breed social ferment, and for Algeria it came in the form of fundamentalism. Sunni sheiks in mosques preached puritanism. They demanded the elimination of government corruption, and the banning of alcohol, beauty parlors, and Western music, as well as mixed sun-bathing at beaches and other mingling of the sexes.

The one-party rulers decided to allow democracy. The first multiparty election was held in 1990 at the municipal level. The new Islamic Salvation Front won overwhelmingly, taking control of more than half of Algeria's cities. Mosques demanded establishment of an Islamic state complete with the grim amputations and floggings required by the *shariá*. Militants took to the streets, attempting to force the closure of bars and beaches. Sun-bathers began avoiding the seashore to escape religious harassment.

By 1991, violence was erupting. Mosques broadcast calls for a holy uprising. Street fighting flared between Muslim extremists and soldiers, causing 100 deaths. Thousands were arrested, and martial law was imposed. Tanks rolled into the capital, Algiers. A curfew was imposed, parliamentary elections were postponed, and political rallies were banned. Insurrectionist sermons in mosques took their place. Preaching to worshipers in a mosque, Islamic Salvation Front leader Abassi Madani threatened to launch a *jihad*. He was arrested on charges of "fomenting an armed conspiracy against the security of the state."

When the parliamentary election was reset for late 1991, the fundamentalists campaigned on the slogan: "No constitution and no laws. The only rule is the Koran and the law of Allah." On election day, they again won overwhelmingly. Algerian newspapers called it "an earthquake." Writer Jill Smolowe said in a January 1992 report that the victory brought "doomsday visions of an Algeria cloaked in black robes and veils, a Koran clutched in one hand, the other the clenched fist of religious fanaticism." About 300,000 secular-minded Algerians marched through Algiers chanting "no to fundamentalism."

Rather than see Algeria become a theocracy, generals ousted the civilian government, voided the election, and took control. They outlawed the Islamic Salvation Front and forbade nonreligious activity in Algeria's ten thousand mosques. Fundamentalist terrorism exploded. Street fighting between extremists and soldiers killed about 1,000 in 1992. Bombings, rioting, and mass arrests were common. In mid-1992, Mohamed Boudiaf, chief of the military-backed ruling council, was assassinated in a machine-gun attack. One of the arrested killers told police he acted "out of religious conviction." In fundamentalist neighborhoods of Algiers, grafitti proclaimed, "Divine justice at work" and "Boudiaf was the devil."

In 1993, former Prime Minister Kasdi Merbah, who

Riot police clash with the Islamic Salvation Front as Muslim fundamentalists protest the removal of Islamic insignias from public buildings. (AP/Wide World Photos)

had urged compromise with the fanatics, was killed in an ambush along with his son, his brother, and two others. For this and other attacks, the government executed more than 100 militants, but it didn't slow the rebellion. The death toll passed 2,000.

Fundamentalist gunmen in 1993 began killing foreign diplomats and foreigners who worked in Algeria's oil industry. Embassies sent staffs home and foreign corporations withdrew many employees.

Zealots wiped out alcohol in Blida, thirty miles south of Algiers, by burning clubs and killing bar owners. Beauty parlors were wrecked. When wall graffiti vowed death to unveiled women, many women in poor sectors fearfully began wearing veils in public.

Writers and other intellectuals who opposed a theocracy were murdered. In the eastern city of Taher, gunmen entered a school, stood a teacher before a blackboard, shot him in the face, then wrote *jihad* on the blackboard and left. Mahfoudh Boucebsi, an internationally known psychiatrist who advocated abortion, was killed by religious assassins. Higher Education Minister Djillali Lyabes, head of a scholarly institute, met the same fate. His successor, sociologist M'hammed Boukhobza, died horribly: fundamentalist gunmen entered his home, tied up his daughter, and made her watch as they cut the professor's throat. A French businessman and his son were killed the same way as their respective families watched in horror. Other terrorists disguised themselves as students, entered the Algiers art academy, and murdered painter Ahmed Asselah and his son. Popular playwright

Abdelkader Alloula was assassinated by a bullet in the head. Numerous journalists also were killed.

Terrorists stormed a prison in 1994 and freed hundreds of militants. Soldiers and police fought the escapees in a mini-war that killed dozens. While the roundup of prisoners was in progress, Muslim fanatics burst into an Algiers newspaper office and opened fire with automatic weapons, killing two newsmen and wounding three. In a March 1994 Associated Press report, Prime Minister Redha Malek called it "an act of inquisition from the Middle Ages, which made intelligence and knowledge its target."

About 50,000 Algerians marched to protest the rise of fundamentalism. The demonstration was led by unveiled women defying the death threats. Unions called a strike against the violence. A week after the march, militants on a motorcycle shot and killed two unveiled high school girls as they waited at an Algiers bus stop. A short time later, as intellectuals and feminists held another march, a fanatic hurled grenades and sprayed gunfire, killing one marcher and wounding 63. Feminist leader Khalida Messaoudi was hit by shrapnel. The Armed Islamic Group boasted that it staged the attack to punish "enemies of the faith." The group also sent assassins to kill a Catholic priest and a nun in an Algiers library where they worked. After the murders, the organization announced that it had a "policy of liquidation" of Christians and Jews.

Other fundamentalist killers slipped aboard an Italian merchant ship moored at the port city of Jijel and cut the throats of seven sailors.

A week later, terrorists stopped a bus, removed five

East European oil workers, forced them to kneel, and killed them. The murders were part of a fundamentalist campaign to drive foreigners from the Muslim nation. The same day, gunmen opened fire at a zoo, killing two Yugoslavians and two Algerians. An hour later, two government education officials were assassinated at their homes. The following day, a gunbattle outside the Italian Embassy in Algiers killed four.

The death toll passed 4,000 by mid-1994, as anti-terrorism courts sentenced 420 militants to death in a year. International observers warned of a possible victory by the fanatics. Thousands of soldiers reportedly deserted and took their guns to join rebels in the southern mountains. Ruling generals increasingly were isolated in guarded seaside compounds. Police and soldiers abandoned villages and slums at night, giving the extremists free rein.

Today, religion in Algeria is as gory as it was 3,000 years ago.

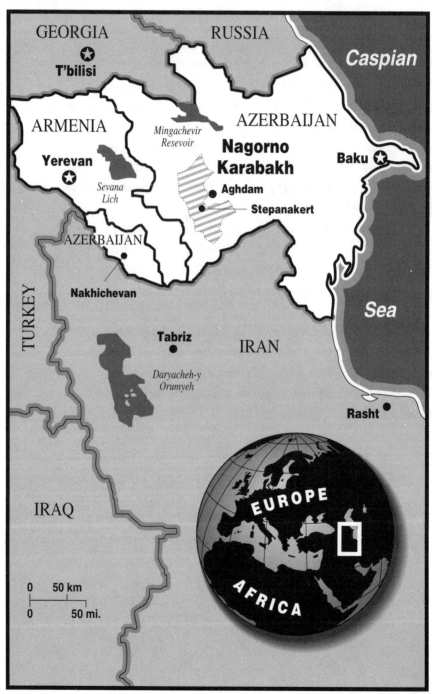

Bill Pitzer- PITZOGraphics

11

The Caucasus

Armenian Christians are like people under a curse. They seem doomed to eternal religious and ethnic conflicts with their neighbors. Thus far in the 1990s, the curse has cost 15,000 lives and caused a million people to flee as refugees. But it's merely the latest episode in 1,700 years of trouble.

Armenia is a little nation in the Caucasus, the mountain isthmus between the Black Sea and the Caspian Sea, just northeast of Turkey. People of the region are perfect examples of the white race—at least according to eighteenth-century German anthropologist Johann Blumenbach, who applied the label *Caucasian* to one of the major divisions of humanity.

Armenia, once a much larger kingdom, was the first Christian nation—a circumstance that has caused recurring problems. In the third century, rulers of neighboring

Persia (now Iran) decreed their official state religion to be Zoroastrianism, the ancient faith in which Magi holy men pray to Ahura Mazda before the Sacred Fire. When Persia conquered Armenia, Zoroastrianism was imposed on the Armenians. But the Armenian king Tiridates III obtained Roman help and drove out the Persians. Tiridates was converted to Christianity in the year 303 and decreed it to be Armenia's only religion, two decades before Constantine made it the official church of the Roman Empire. People who had prayed to Ahura Mazda began praying to the Christian trinity. Efforts were made to stamp out Zoroastrianism.

Persia overran Armenia again and attempted to reimpose Zoroastrianism. Then fanatical Arabs swept both countries in the 600s while spreading the new religion of Islam by the sword. Most Persians became Muslim, but Armenians remained Christian. (Zoroastrianism survived in small pockets. Today it is still practiced by about 18,000 Iranians and by more than 100,000 Parsees in India.)

Throughout its history, many conquerors held Armenia. During the various occupations, thousands of Armenians scattered as refugees. In the 1500s, Muslim Turks took over and treated the Christians as inferiors. The Armenians looked to Orthodox Russia for help, which precipitated conflict. In the 1850s, the czar declared Russia the protector of Christians and holy places in the Turkish Ottoman Empire. The sultan replied with gunfire, and the Crimean War began. The czar appealed to Christian nations for help in fighting the Muslims, but Britain and

France sent troops to support the sultan. Most of the combat occurred in the small Crimean peninsula in the Black Sea west of the Caucasus. Despite the slaughter of Britain's Light Brigade, immortalized in Tennyson's poem, the allies won, and Russia was forced to make humiliating concessions.

In the late 1800s, Western missionaries roused religious ferment among Armenians in Turkey, which turned into agitation for independence. Protests and riots occurred, followed by massacres of Armenians. More than 200,000 were reported killed in the 1890s and early 1900s. During World War I, in which Turkey sided with Germany, Armenians rebelled and slaughtered Turks. The Muslims struck back with ferocious killing that continued after the war. Charges of genocide have been raised ever since, but some historians say the conflict killed more Muslims than Christians.

A 1920 treaty set Armenia free of Turkish rule, but Bolshevik troops quickly seized it for the new Soviet Union. For six decades, Communist might suppressed religious and ethnic differences in the Caucasus. But as the Red empire began to disintegrate, old hostilities resurfaced between Christian Armenians and their Muslim neighbors, the Azerbaijanis. The trouble centered on the enclave of Nagorno-Karabakh, home of 100,000 Christians inside the Muslim land.

In 1988, Armenians in the enclave began demanding union with Armenia. Riots and killing broke out. Armenia expelled 200,000 Muslims. Azerbaijan expelled 260,000 Christians. Guerrilla groups grew on both sides. In 1989,

Azerbaijan, bordering the Caspian Sea, imposed a blockade on Armenia, which was landlocked in the mountains. In 1990, bombings and assassinations continued.

Soviet army units arrived as peacekeepers but wound up massacring Muslim protesters in Azerbaijan. Neighboring Iran sympathized with the Muslims, and was accused of arming them. Iran's former interior minister warned that the Soviet troops faced retribution from "resistance cells" that were "lying in ambush for the enemies of Islam." Jews of the Caucasus, fearing that the religious hate would soon turn on them, began fleeing to Israel.

Armenia declared independence from the crumbling Soviet Union in 1990, and made itself controller of the Christian Nagorno-Karabakh enclave inside Azerbaijan. But the Muslim nation refused to yield the territory. When Azerbaijan declared independence from the Soviet Union in 1991, it, too, asserted ownership of Nagorno-Karabakh. Then Christians in the enclave declared their own independence from Azerbaijan. All the while, terrorist attacks and guerrilla clashes were rising, killed more people.

Christian rebels overran the Muslim town of Khojaly in 1992 and massacred its people: victims were burned, scalped, beheaded, and otherwise mutilated. Witnesses said corpses of women and children covered a hillside. Armenian offensives captured Azerbaijani territory, opening two pathways to the disputed enclave. Worsening defeats caused the new Azerbaijani government to fall.

By 1993, Christians had seized all of the enclave, plus all the land separating it from Armenia. The death toll had reached 15,000, with a million refugees fleeing in all directions. Some of the refugee families froze to death trying to cross mountain passes in winter. Repeated Muslim sabotage severed railways and gas pipelines to Armenia.

In 1994, a terrorist bomb blew up the subway in the Azerbaijani capital of Baku, killing twelve people and injuring dozens. Armenian Christian saboteurs were blamed.

After six years of combat, the region of the civil war has been devastated. Thousands of buildings have been shattered, electricity and water have failed, fuel is lacking, food is scarce, telephones don't work, hospitals can't function, factories and schools are destroyed or closed. People who enjoyed full employment under communism are suddenly suffering overwhelming joblessness. There's no gasoline for cars. Trees have been mowed down for firewood. Groups huddle in basements, telling relief agencies they're starving and freezing.

What a terrible price for Muslims and Christians to pay for their inability to live as neighbors.

12

Israel

The half-century conflict between Jewish Israelis and their Muslim neighbors is basically a struggle over land. Yet a river of religion runs through it. The river swelled in the 1990s as religion loomed larger in Israel's violence. Rising Islamic fundamentalism among Palestinians—in Israel proper, in the Occupied Territories, and in refugee camps in nearby nations—altered the terrorism.

The former source of terror, the aging Palestine Liberation Organization (PLO), never was known especially for Muslim fanaticism. (Chairman Yassir Arafat married a young Christian in 1991.) The PLO signed a historic peace agreement in 1993 and renounced violence. However, its old goal of exterminating the Jewish state was adopted by young religious militants in *Hezbollah* (the Party of God), in *Hamas* (an acronym for Islamic Resistance

Movement meaning "zeal" in Arabic), in Islamic *Jihad* (Holy War), and the like. They committed endless shootings, stabbings, and bombings while Israeli soldiers inflicted countless reprisals.

At the same time, murder was committed by the worst zealots among Jews, many of whom contend that no part of Israel should be surrendered to Arabs, because God gave the land to the Jews.

Clashes of belief always are magnified in Jerusalem, a city deemed holy by Jews, Muslims, and Christians. Israeli writer Amos Elon calls the city a "civic embodiment of contentious faiths."* On the dustjacket of Elon's book *Jerusalem: City of Mirrors,* playwright Arthur Miller called Jerusalem "a compressed symbol of our most sublime aspirations along with our most disgusting, hatefully brainless excursions into religious bigotry and fratricide."

In the 1989 book Elon said some fervent pilgrims to the city are overcome by what local psychiatrists call "Jerusalem syndrome." He said it affects mostly Americans who "have a strong grounding in the Bible. In Jerusalem, they suddenly take off their clothes or shout prophecies on street corners, only to revert to normal after a few days' treatment."†

Sigmund Freud once wrote to a friend just back from Jerusalem: "How strange this tragically mad land you have visited must have seemed to you. It has never produced anything but religions, sacred frenzies, presumptuous

---

Newsweek, May 14, 1990, p. 34.

†From a review of *Jerusalem* by Christopher Lehmann-Haupt in the *New York Times.*

attempts to overcome the outer world of appearances by means of the inner world of wishful thinking."

The behavior of visiting pilgrims is mild compared to that of Jerusalem's residents. Ever since Israel seized the city in the Six-Day War in 1967—the third of its four wars with Muslims—trouble has seethed between religious sectors of town. Jews were jubilant at regaining their ancient biblical capital, and exerted constant pressure to take over the whole city. The Jerusalem Reclamation Project, based in New York, raised money to buy Muslim homes in Jerusalem in an effort to Judaize the city. Muslim and Christian residents of Jerusalem resisted.

The epicenter of conflict is the Temple Mount, a thirty-five-acre height where the temples of Solomon and Herod stood. In the year 70 C.E., Roman legions defeated Jewish rebels and burned the Second Temple. Surviving Jews were dispersed across the Roman Empire, ending the Jewish state for 1,900 years. Of the temple, all that remained was one wall, which later became the Wailing Wall of Jewish laments. Muslims say Muhammad ascended to heaven on horseback from the Temple Mount, leaping into the sky from a flat rock in which they discern a hoofprint. They built the ornate Dome of the Rock mosque over the sacred stone, and also built the al-Aqsa mosque nearby.

After Jerusalem's 1967 recapture, some ardent Jews plotted to destroy the mosques and rebuild the temple. Oddly, they received financial support from American Christian fundamentalists who think restoration of the temple would fulfill Bible prophecy, boding the return of Jesus, the conversion of the Jews, the Battle of Armageddon, and so forth. In 1983, Israeli police caught forty Jewish fanatics with Uzi weapons and explosives trying to break through tunnels under the mosques on Temple Mount.

In 1990, about 150 armed Jewish zealots awaiting the messiah moved into four buildings in Jerusalem's Christian quarter, triggering an international protest by Christian and Muslim groups. Later, it was discovered that the Israeli Ministry of Housing had put up $1.5 million in public funds to acquire the buildings.

Then came the Temple Mount massacre in late 1990. A Muslim rumor spread that Jews were preparing to lay a cornerstone for the third temple. Many Muslims ran to a mosque, where a loudspeaker exhorted them to defend the sacred site. A mob swarmed to the top of the mount and flung rocks at Jews praying at the Wailing Wall below. Israeli police first fired tear gas, then rubber bullets, and finally real bullets: 19 Muslims were killed and 140 wounded. The incident triggered riots and killings throughout Israel. Two weeks later in Jerusalem, a Muslim teen-ager screaming "God is great!" stabbed to death three Jews, including an eighteen-year-old female soldier. This sent Jewish throngs into the streets, stoning Muslim cars and beating Muslim pedestrians.

Meanwhile, the *intifada* (Arabic for "uprising") was raging in Palestinian towns in the Occupied Territories (the West Bank, the Golan Heights, and the Gaza Strip). Muslim teen-agers threw rocks and Molotov cocktails. Israeli troops replied with gunfire. The death toll climbed to more than 1,000. Soldiers used increasingly oppressive tactics, such as sending bulldozers to crush the family

Israeli Arabs protest Israel's killing of 19 Arabs on the Temple Mount. (Reuters/Bettmann)

A Palestinian woman kisses a handprint on a wall of the Temple Mount. These prints were made from the blood of those killed. (Reuters/Bettmann)

homes of rock-throwers. The religious factor in the *intifada* was visible in a 1989 incident: A young Muslim, riding in a bus laden with Jews, screamed "God is great!" and jerked the steering wheel, sending the bus plunging 200 feet into a ravine. Fourteen people were killed and 27 injured, including the Muslim.

Islamic fundamentalist groups assumed leadership of the violent resistance, undercutting the authority of the PLO. For example, in 1992, Muslim terrorists slipped into an Israeli army camp and hacked three soldiers to death with knives and axes. The killers were Israeli citizens who secretly belonged to Islamic *Jihad*, the outlawed branch of *Hezbollah*, the Iran-linked Shi'ite militia operating throughout the Middle East. Israel retaliated by sending jet fighters to strike a motorcade carrying *Hezbollah* leader Abbas Musawi in south Lebanon: the holy man, his wife and child were killed. The assassination triggered more Muslim attacks. According to a newswire report dated February 16, 1992, fellow Sheik Mohammed Fadlallah ordered "all resistance fighters to escalate their *jihad* against Israel." The same newswire reported on February 20 that *Hezbollah* guerrillas—some wearing "God is great!" headbands—fired rockets at Israeli bases. Israel retaliated with commando raids.

Soon afterward, a large car bomb shattered the Israeli Embassy in Buenos Aires, Argentina, killing more than 28 people and wounding 220. Islamic *Jihad* announced in Beirut that a Muslim suicide bomber gave his life in the blast to avenge the "martyred" Musawi. It said such strikes would continue "until Israel is wiped out of existence."

In the Gaza Strip, Palestinian children hold toy guns in the air in support of the *intifada.* (Larry Towell/Magnum Photos)

In late 1992, after six Israeli soldiers were killed in ten days, Israel deported 415 Muslims suspected of secret membership in Islamic *Jihad* and *Hamas*. Lebanon refused to accept them, and the 415 were kept in a freezing camp in a buffer zone between the two nations. Rioting and killing erupted over the expulsion.

Israeli leaders, conducting intensive peace talks with the PLO and heads of Arab states, feared that the rising religious fervor would erode accomplishments at the negotiating table. Benyamin Begin, son of Israel's former prime minister, was quoted in the *Washington Post* as warning of "the surge of Islamic fundamentalism. It is a very dangerous phenomenon that has jumped from Iran over Iraq to Jordan; over Egypt to Sudan; over Syria to Lebanon; and even into Gaza, Judea, and Samaria."

But fundamentalism isn't limited to Muslims. Some of Israel's ultra-orthodox Jews are known for puritanism and intolerance. The nation's Chief Rabbinate, which sets kosher rules for restaurants, attempted to revoke the licenses of clubs employing belly dancers. But a popular dancer appealed to Israel's Supreme Court, which ruled in 1990 that the rabbis can't dictate entertainment. Scientist Israel Shahak told the *Washington Report on Middle East Affairs* in a 1990 interview that some Israeli Orthodox Jews hate Christians so much that they devised a different symbol to replace the "plus" sign in mathematics because it resembles a Christian cross.

Territorial theology is strong among Jews living in settlements in the occupied West Bank and Gaza Strip, surrounded by Muslims. They contend that God gave the

Promised Land to Jews, and it mustn't be traded away in peace negotiations.

As Israeli and PLO chiefs neared a long-awaited treaty in 1993, both Muslim and Jewish extremists called their leaders traitors. Wall slogans calling for holy murder of Jews sprouted in the Occupied Territories. Speakers in mosques endorsed holy war. Fundamentalist rabbis declared that yielding any of the land conquered in the 1967 war would betray the biblical vision of greater Israel. Violent clashes and terrorist incidents increased.

Hamas members also killed Muslims they suspected of seeking compromise with Israel. When PLO ally Tawfiq Hosa called for a halt to the "collaborator killings," in September 1993, *Newsweek* reported that *Hamas* agents brought two bound captives to his doorstep, shot them, and left their bodies as a "gift" for him.

(And the fanatics killed Muslim women accused of "licentiousness," or of dishonoring their men by sexual straying. Like all Muslims, the Palestinians impose severe strictures on females. In an Associated Press report dated February 14, 1994, the Israeli human rights group Betselem stated that the deaths of 107 Palestinian women during the *intifada* were "honor killings" to avenge sexual impurity. Even rape victims who became pregnant were killed.)

The peace treaty was signed in Washington on September 13, tentatively granting Palestinians a homeland in the Gaza Strip and in the West Bank city of Jericho. Militants reacted fiercely. At a New York synagogue, fundamentalist Jews threw eggs at Israel's ambassador, and some pickets carried signs saying the treaty was a betrayal because "the Messiah is coming." In Gaza, as some Muslims cheered the treaty, young *Hamas* members flailing clubs and chains broke up rallies. Jewish settlers surrounded by Muslims in the Occupied Territories felt betrayed. *Time* magazine reported in September of 1993 that former Chief Rabbi Shlomo Goren told them that any Jew who meets PLO leader Yassir Arafat "has the right to kill him." Muslim fanatics also vowed to kill Arafat. Hard-liners called for "a day of wrath" on all parties to the treaty.

Among sporadic killings that followed the treaty signing, an Israeli bus driver was stabbed to death. Islamic *Jihad* claimed responsibility and said: "Yesterday's attack with Allah's knife was to say no to the surrender—no to the signing of the Gaza-Jericho agreement—no to the recognition of the security and safety of the Zionist traitors." *Hamas* leaflets called the signing "the blackest day in Islamic history." On the Jewish side, members of the fundamentalist Kach party protested and were arrested to prevent violence. Many among the 130,000 Jewish settlers in the Occupied Territories cited Bible passages to prove that God intended for Jews to have the land. The Associated Press reported on February 14, 1994, that when Muslim teen-agers threw stones in the West Bank town of El Bireh, near Jericho, troops stormed into a high school and killed a poet's son with a bullet in the stomach.

The months following the treaty were marred by numerous killings and counter-killings, riots, and fire-bombings. In the December 6, 1993, issue of *Newsweek* it was reported that at Ben Gurion Airport, police arrested a fundamentalist rabbi attempting to smuggle in silencers and bomb-making equipment. In Gaza, Israeli undercover agents killed a twenty-four-year-old *Hamas* leader wanted for killing eleven soldiers. The terrorist, Imad Aqal, had told friends he wanted to be a martyr for Allah, "to go to paradise by being killed by Israeli soldiers." He got his wish. A *Hamas* song declares: "Don't cry for me, Mother. Let my blood flow. I'm going to paradise."

While the Occupied Territories seethed, *Hezbollah* militants and Israeli troops conducted dozens of gory raids and reprisals along Lebanon's southern border. *Hezbollah* attacks brought Israeli shelling of border towns, killing civilians. One week-long barrage in mid-1993 killed 147. Israeli commandos swept into the border zone in 1994 and seized the leader of a different religious terrorist group, the Believers Resistance.

In early 1994, Jewish soldiers began withdrawing from Gaza as required by the peace treaty. Hundreds of Jewish settlers, not wanting to remain unguarded in a sea of Muslims, sought to leave the new Islamic homeland.

Then came a shock felt around the world: In the ancient West Bank city of Hebron, a fundamentalist Jewish settler with an automatic weapon entered a temple and killed thirty Muslims as they prayed, foreheads to the floor, during their holy Ramadan season. Outraged worshipers beat him to death.

This horror happened in a famed shrine over a cave where Abraham and Sarah were buried. It's the only building in the world where Jews and Muslims worship

(*above*) The Cave of the Patriarchs in Hebron, where Dr. Baruch Goldstein (*left*) opened fire on Palestinian worshipers in a mosque, killing 20 and wounding at least 65 before being overtaken and killed himself. (Reuters/ Bettmann)

together, usually in shifts, but sometimes simultaneously. Both Jews and Muslims revere Abraham as a patriarch.

The assassin was an American-born doctor, Baruch Goldstein, an ardent member of an ultrareligious New York family. "He was very distant because he was so religious," a neighbor recalled. While in college, he had joined Rabbi Meir Kahane's militant Jewish Defense League before moving to Israel and becoming active in Kahane's Kach party.

As a settler in a Hebron kibbutz, Dr. Goldstein treated Jews wounded by Muslims and grew increasingly bitter. On the night before the massacre he had tried to pray at the shared temple, but jeering Muslims interrupted him. The next morning he read his children a passage from the Book of Esther including: "Thus the Jews smote all their enemies . . . and did what they would to those that hated them." Then he armed himself with a 750-shot-per-minute assault weapon, went to the shrine, and unleashed horror.

The massacre virtually wrecked the peace treaty. Enraged Muslims rose in stone-throwing outbursts, and Jewish soldiers shot many protesters. Violence between civilian groups surged. A Muslim who lived near a Jewish enclave found his car smashed, and a note in Hebrew saying "God's Revenge Organization."

Extremist Jews deemed Dr. Goldstein a hero and a martyr. They saw symbolism in the fact that the slaughter happened at the feast of Purim, celebrating an ancient Jewish victory over Persian oppressors. "He could not have picked a better day—the first day of Purim—a day when the Jews fight back," said an American chief of the Kahane movement.*

But Israeli Prime Minister Yitzhak Rabin called the doctor a "degenerate murderer" who "grew in a swamp" that included "false messianic claims." Addressing Israel's Knesset, Rabin said: "A single straight line connects the lunatics and racists of the entire world. A single line of blood and terrorism runs from the Islamic *Jihad* member who shot Jewish worshipers as they stood in prayer in the synagogues of Istanbul, Paris, Amsterdam, and Rome, to the Jewish *Hamas* member [Goldstein] who shot Ramadan worshipers."† The infuriated prime minister meant that Dr. Goldstein was the equivalent of a Muslim *Hamas* murderer.

Israeli leaders tried to quell the violence by abolishing militant Jewish groups, disarming some extremists, and temporarily banning worship at the Wailing Wall to avert confrontations. But the conflict and killing continued. Some extremist Jews went underground, as Muslim fanatics had done previously.

In late March of 1994, the Associated Press reported that *Hamas* militants came to Hebron, planning revenge on Jewish settlers. Hundreds of troops surrounded their building and killed them with a twenty-two-hour fusillade of 100 anti-tank rockets and tens of thousands of bullets. This incident, like the others, triggered more Muslim upheaval.

Newsweek, March 7, 1994, p. 35.
†*Near East Report*, March 14, 1994, p. 42.

A month after the mosque massacre, a Muslim suicide bomber detonated an explosive-packed car beside a bus picking up Jewish junior high school students. Eight people were killed and 44 wounded. Mosque loudspeakers in Gaza City announced *Hamas* boasts of the "heroic" attack. A week later, another bus bombing killed six.

A West Bank Jewish settler named Daniel Diker told reporters, "People don't understand. This isn't just over land. It's a religious war—it's Islam versus Judaism."*

The religious war spirit was magnified when on May 10, 1994, Yassir Arafat, speaking at a South African mosque, called for a Muslim *jihad* to "liberate" Jerusalem and make it the capital of a new Palestinian state.

As if Israel didn't have enough religious problems, members of a charismatic Jewish cult barricaded themselves in a compound in a Tel Aviv suburb in 1994. Armed with submachine guns, the cultists—followers of the appropriately named Rabbi Uzi Meshulam—crouched behind sandbag walls and held police at bay for six weeks. The siege ended after a fierce gunbattle in which one cultist was killed. The rest surrendered.

Killings by Muslim militants, Jewish settlers, and Israeli soldiers continued weekly through much of mid-1994. Former Chief Rabbi Goren renewed his call for the assassination of Arafat, and also urged Jews living on the West Bank to "fight to the death" before surrendering the territory to Muslims. An Arafat aide told Israeli reporters that Goren is crazy.

The New York Times, March 3, 1994.

Meanwhile, another terrorism tragedy occurred, apparently stemming from the gory strife with *Hezbollah* militants in south Lebanon. In June, Israeli aircraft struck a *Hezbollah* village and killed 50 people. Leaders of the Islamic militia vowed "swift and merciless" retaliation. A month later, a Jewish charity building in Buenos Aires was demolished by a huge explosion that killed nearly 100 occupants. The following day, an airliner over Panama was destroyed by a bomb, killing 21 people, 12 of whom were Jewish businessmen. In south Lebanon, a group calling itself *Ansarollah* (Partisans of God) claimed credit, announcing: "Suicide martyr squads have been formed to confront and combat Zionism everywhere. The Argentine and Panama Operations are evidence of this continuing confrontation."* A week later, two more car bombs exploded in London, one outside the Israeli Embassy, the other outside a Jewish charity. Nineteen people were injured, but none killed.

Prime Minister Rabin blamed *Hezbollah* and its sponsor, Iran. He called on democratic nations to join forces and "strike at this viper and crush its skull." Iran's chief cleric, Ayatollah Ali Khamenei, replied fiercely that Israel is a "counterfeit" nation, a "cancerous tumor inside an Islamic body," and a "gathering of a bunch of Jews from around the world who possess qualities such as mischief, malice, thievery, and murder." He added: "Because of their filthy nature, the Zionists have no right to adjudicate on Islamic Iran."*

---

*Associated Press, July 20, 1994.
*Ibid.

The hatred in this language lends insight into the religious-political-ethnic nightmare from which the Middle East cannot awaken.

13

Muslim Horror

As the Cold War recedes into history, some observers fear that Muslim violence is replacing it as the new international peril.

The *London Sunday Times* warned in November of 1990: "Almost every month, the threat from the Warsaw Pact diminishes; but every year, for the rest of this decade and beyond, the threat from fundamentalist Islam will grow. . . . The West will have to learn how to contain it, just as it once had to learn how to contain Soviet Communism."

Life magazine commented in March 1993: "Today, after the disintegration of communism, Islam represents the last great monolith of militant belief and, to many Westerners, the most coherent threat to the new world order."

155

Author Leon Uris said he wrote *The Hajj*, his novel about Islam, to warn the West "that we have an enraged bull of a billion people on our planet, and tilted the wrong way they could open the second road to Armageddon."*

Italy's news magazine *Europeo* said in March 1992 that poverty, corruption, and joblessness in Muslim nations were "smoothing the way for 'God's fanatics' from the Maghreb to Western Asia."

Leonard Spector of the Carnegie Endowment for International Peace wrote in a 1993 issue of the *Economist*: "The spread of nuclear weapons through the Islamic world will be a principal strategic concern of the West for the rest of this century."

(Imagine the horror if the rental van parked in the World Trade Center had contained a smuggled nuclear device instead of homemade fertilizer explosive. Or imagine the tragedy, while the United States was crushing Iraq in the Persian Gulf War, if Iraqi President Saddam Hussein could have sent a pleasure boat containing a hidden nuclear bomb up the Potomac River into the heart of Washington.)

Here's another sign that Islam is replacing communism as the menace of the 1990s: Novelist Tom Clancy, who sold millions of copies of his five thrillers about Cold War intrigues, switched topics in his sixth novel, *The Sum of All Fears*. His new peril is the conflict between Muslims and Jews in the Middle East.

However, some scholars say the fundamentalist threat

*Daniel Pipes, *National Review*, November 19, 1900, p. 28.

is partly illusory. Islamic expert Daniel Pipes of Philadelphia says Muslim nations and groups have too many inner conflicts ever to pose a unified danger to the West. The majority of Muslims are as humane and peaceful as other people, he says, and only a few feel enough hostility to turn violent.

Leon Hadar, former bureau chief of the *Jerusalem Post*, stated in *Policy Analysis*, "the numerous cultural, political and economic divisions in the Islamic world preclude Islamic fundamentalism's becoming an effective monolithic movement."* He and others concur that the fanatics pose a greater threat to their own nations than to the outside world.

Whichever view is correct, it's clear that religion-related killing and cruelty are frequent problems in Muslim areas, especially when Muslims come into contact with rival faiths. In some cases, the blame lies as much with the rivals as with the Muslims.

What follows is a thumbnail account of holy hatred involving Muslims in nations not covered by other chapters of this book:

Afghanistan

First, this backward mountain nation suffered a communist takeover. Then it suffered a fundamentalist takeover. The first was bad, but the second was ghastly.

---

*August 27, 1992.

Afghanistan—a harsh realm where temperatures can go from freezing at dawn to 100 degrees at noon, where life expectancy barely exceeds forty years, where 90 percent of the people are illiterate, where 80,000 starved in a three-year drought in the 1960s—has suffered 2 million deaths in a fifteen-year holy war that turned into a killing feud between fundamentalist rivals. Three million were wounded while 5 million became refugees.

In 1978, young Marxist military officers shot their way to power and began imposing "modernity" on the hidebound Muslim society. Unveiled women went to universities, and other liberations of "scientific socialism" occurred. Rural Muslim tribes rebelled against this "satanic" Western trend. (It wasn't their first such uprising. In the 1920s, a young king named Amanullah decreed modern reforms, but *mullah* holy men incited a gory rebellion that toppled him.)

The Marxists fought among themselves, and hordes of *mujahideen* (holy warriors) from the hills were gaining the upper hand, so the Soviet Red Army invaded in 1979 to avert a fundamentalist victory. Mass executions were held. Savage war ensued for a decade.

From Washington the CIA covertly armed and supplied the rebels, making them surrogates in the Cold War against Moscow. Most aid went to the *Hezb-i-Islami* faction led by Gulbuddin Hekmatyar, who had leaped to fundamentalist leadership as a young man by throwing acid in the faces of college girls who didn't wear veils.*

---

*Richard Reeves, *The New York Times*, October 14, 1990.

As the war raged through the 1980s, Hekmatyar's fanatics often killed rival Muslim guerrillas while at the same time killing Soviet troops. Atrocities were committed by all sides. Muslim zealots from several nations flocked to Afghanistan to fight in the *jihad*. By 1989, the Soviets had suffered 30,000 casualties and realized the war was futile. The Red Army withdrew, leaving the Communist Afghan regime to fight on alone. It survived three years, bottled up in major cities. Urban people were slaughtered by endless *mujahideen* assaults. Finally, in 1992, the Communists surrendered to a council of Muslim rebels.

But the holy warriors quickly began killing each other. Internecine war flared when a Sunni militia clashed with a Shi'ite militia, and when Hekmatyar felt cheated by being named only prime minister rather than president of the new government, he and other dissident leaders were driven out of the capital, Kabul. They inflicted ruthless bombardment and aircraft attacks on the city's helpless citizens, then recaptured parts of Kabul. Thousands died in the fighting between Muslim units.

By 1994, six different rebel factions held parts of the capital, which was by now in ruins. Food, water, electricity, heat, and other essentials were lost. About 30,000 people were taking shelter in schools, mosques, and offices in Kabul. Many were freezing and starving.

Across the border in neighboring Pakistan, hundreds of Afghan women staged a march seeking removal of all the rival Muslim chiefs. Some carried banners calling the leaders "fundamentalist terrorists."

Also in 1994, three masked Afghan terrorists in

Pakistan seized a busload of Pakistani teachers and schoolboys, and demanded that 2,000 truckloads of food be sent to the desperate people of Kabul. They held their hostages in the Afghan Embassy at Islamabad. Pakistani commandos stormed the embassy, killed the fanatics, and rescued the hostages. A freed teacher told news reporters: "It was God who saved us."

Amnesty International stated in its 1993 annual report that one of the first actions taken by Muslim leaders after the Communist surrender in Afghanistan was to impose the *shariá* religious law. The justice ministry decreed that adulterers would be stoned to death, thieves would have a hand or foot severed, anyone drinking alcohol would suffer eighty lashes, and anyone selling alcohol would be put to death.

Somalia

Oppression of women, a blight in all Muslim societies, reaches its worst stage in Somalia, the East African nation ravaged by clan warfare in the 1990s. Although Somali women aren't forced to wear veils and shrouds, nearly all of them are genitally mutilated to dull their sexual pleasure and keep them "pure" for husbands in this male-dominated culture.

Globally, female circumcision, as it is sometimes called, is inflicted each year on an estimated two million pre-pubescent girls, most of whom are members of African Muslim tribes, but some can be found in the Middle East and in Asia. The girls are held down, usually by their mothers and village females, while their clitorises are cut away with knives, razors, or broken glass. In many cases, their vaginas are sewn partly shut. The goal is to guarantee that they remain virgins until married.

When United Nations peacekeeping troops went to Somalia to stop the clan slaughter, the Western world was horrified by mutilation reports that filtered back. An outcry was raised for human rights action to protect Muslim women.

Despite their desexed condition, some Somali women are accused of adultery, and are killed for it. In 1993, in the northern city of Hargeisa, U.N. observers found a throng of fundamentalists stoning five women to death and flogging a sixth. The stoners weren't primitive tribesmen; some of them videotaped the killing. The U.N. agents tried to stop it, but were driven off by threats of stoning.

United Nations official Cecilia Kamau said Muslim leaders had sentenced the five to death for engaging in sex, but the sixth received only flogging because she was unmarried. Worshipers imposed the punishment after Friday prayers in a mosque. "It would seem that fundamentalism is really catching on," Ms. Kamau told reporters, adding that U.N. employees feared harm from the fanatics.*

News reports made no mention of any punishment for the men who had sex with the women. Evidently,

---

*The Associated Press, January 18, 1993.

161

fundamentalist Muslims consider sex a capital offense only for women.

Somalia, occupying the eastern "horn" of Africa, is a backward land where three-fourths of the people can't read, and where the annual gross product per person is worth merely $170. The population is 99 percent Muslim and intolerant of other beliefs.

In 1994, Christian groups trying to help hungry Somalis were attacked by Muslim extremists. Grenades were thrown into offices of Catholic Relief Services and an Irish charity. A Muslim clique issued a statement accusing the Christians of proselytizing. "Anyone who tries to distribute anything concerning Christianity will be shot," the statement said.

Saudi Arabia

The birthplace of Islam is so puritanical it's like a religious prison. Women must be cloaked to their eyes in public, and are forbidden to vote, drive cars, or engage in legal actions such as seeking a divorce. They must use separate beaches, movie theaters, and schools. Morality police sometimes beat women considered immodestly dressed, and raid homes suspected of containing alcohol. Religious courts rule with an iron fist, applying the *shariá* law, complete with amputations and beheadings.

For example, a man named Sadeq Malallah was beheaded in the marketplace of Qatif in 1992 after being convicted of "insulting Allah, the Holy Koran, and Muhammad the Prophet."* In 1993, some Saudi intellectuals formed a human rights group to advocate free speech, but they had to flee for their lives after the *Ulema* (a board of holy scholars) declared them enemies of Islam. Amnesty International said in its 1993 report: "Between April and October, eight judicial amputations were carried out in Juddah, Jizan, and other cities. All had their right hands severed at the wrist after being convicted of theft." The human rights group added that a Saudi woman accused of adultery was given 200 lashes.

Unmarried sex is a capital crime—as demonstrated by the famous case of a Saudi princess who was executed for having a lover. (The incident was made into a television movie, which was shown on America's Public Broadcasting System in the 1980s, despite Saudi protests that it slandered Islam.) Yet Saudi men are allowed multiple wives in "marriages" that are hardly partnerships. In 1991, a sixty-year-old Saudi sheik was arrested in India for buying a ten-year-old Indian girl from her impoverished family and marrying her. Police became aware of the marriage because the child began crying on an airliner as the aging sheik prepared to take her home with him.

Saudi Arabia occupies most of the Arabian Peninsula, which Muhammad first united under his bellicose faith in the 600s. Today, one billion Muslims around the world bow five times a day toward Mecca, where the Great Mosque houses a sacred Black Stone, which Muslims think

---

Charleston Daily Mail, October 6, 1992.

the Angel Gabriel handed to Ishmael, Abraham's son who supposedly was the progenitor of all Arabs.

Each year, more than one million Muslims make the *hajj*, a pilgrimage to Mecca, sometimes producing tragedy. In 1994, swarms of believers crammed into a sacred cavern outside Mecca to "stone the devil" (hurl rocks at pillars, as Muhammad supposedly did). Panic caused a stampede that killed 270. Four years earlier, similar panic in a wide tunnel linking Mecca sites killed 1,426. After the 1990 calamity, King Fahd declared: "It was God's will, which is above everything. . . . Had they not died there, they would have died elsewhere and at the same predestined moment." In 1989, two bombs exploded during the *hajj*, killing a pilgrim and wounding others. Saudi authorities later beheaded 16 Kuwaiti Shi'ites as terrorists. The 1989 bombing presumably was in retaliation for a 1987 clash in which Saudi police opened fire, killing 400 Iranian *hajj* pilgrims engaged in a violent protest against "the Great Satan," America. Muslims believe that pilgrims who die at Mecca go immediately to paradise.

The puritanism of Saudi Arabia can be traced to the *Wahhabi* movement. In the 1700s, a holy man named Abd al-Wahhab denounced worldly pleasures and organized the *Ikhwan* (brothers) to fight *jihads* against worldly rulers. The Saud dynasty joined forces with the *Wahhabi* warriors. In nearly two centuries of see-saw warfare, the *Wahhabis* sometimes conquered much of the peninsula, and sometimes were defeated and driven into the desert. Finally, the *Ikhwan* destroyed rival Muslim forces in the 1920s, and made Ibn Saud king. However, *Wahhabi* fanatics soon decided that Saud, too, had become worldly, and rebelled against him. King Saud's army then crushed the holy warriors who had put him in power.

Turkey

Turkey strives to be a secular nation, and elected a woman premier in 1993. But growing fundamentalist terrorism, partly fostered by Iran, plagues the country.

In 1990, a female professor named Bahriye Ucok, who publicly advocated secularism, was killed by a bomb mailed to her home. Three years later, a secular editor, Aziz Nesin, published excerpts from Salman Rushdie's *The Satanic Verses* as a demonstration of free speech. It caused riots in Turkey's seaport city of Istanbul. Two months later, Nesin and other intellectuals held a seminar at the fundamentalist stronghold of Sivas to commemorate a sixteenth-century poet who was hanged for opposing religious oppression. Another riot broke out, and fundamentalists set fire to the hotel where the seminar was held. The fire killed thirty-seven people.

In 1994, police arrested four suspected members of Islamic Action, an underground fundamentalist cell accused of assassinating Turkish politicians and journalists who advocated separation of church and state.

Amid the attacks, the new female prime minister, Tansu Ciller, declared that terrorism will not cause Turkey to become an Islamic theocracy.

The Philippines

As unlikely as it may seem, Muslim terrorists plague the Catholic Philippine Islands. Filipinos are 83 percent Catholic, 9 percent Protestant, and only 5 percent Muslim. The latter mostly belong to the Moro tribe on the large southern island of Mindanao. Twenty years ago, extremists among them began rebelling to establish an Islamic theocracy. The former Marcos dictatorship suppressed the uprising, but it recurred periodically.

In the 1990s, the conflict has taken the form of deadly attacks between Muslims and Catholics. In late 1992, police said an armed band "screaming like demons" raided three remote Christian villages and killed about 40 people. In late 1993, two men pretending to be travelers flagged down a bus. When it stopped, 20 terrorists sprang from bushes and ordered passengers to disembark. They separated Christians from Muslims, then killed nine Christians, including a baby. Oddly, the Muslim killers spared a Christian minister.

Two weeks later, Muslims threw grenades into San Pedro Cathedral at Davao City, killing seven Catholics and wounding 140. In retaliation, grenades exploded at three mosques, injuring five Muslims. Police posted round-the-clock guards at all the city's mosques and churches to avert further attacks.

In the capital, Manila, leaders urged majority Christians not to take revenge on Muslims. "A Christian backlash could turn Mindanao into a Lebanon," said Senator Blas Ople.

In June and July of 1994, a Muslim zealot group called Abu Sayyaf kidnapped Christians and planted bombs in Christian neighborhoods. When an army unit was sent to attack a remote Abu Sayyaf camp on southern Jolo Island, other members abducted 39 more Christians, massacred 15 of them, and held the rest for ransom.

Jordan

This desert kingdom, bordering Israel on the east, is cursed by two types of rising fundamentalism: above-board political campaigning and underground terrorism.

In 1989, King Hussein permitted popular elections. To the surprise of Jordan's educated elite, the puritanical Muslim Brotherhood and other fundamentalists—campaigning on a platform of "Islam is the solution"—grabbed twenty-two seats in parliament, becoming its biggest bloc.

They sought to ban alcohol, halt kissing on Jordanian television, and segregate the sexes. In their hostility to sex they sought to forbid males to watch girls' athletic events at schools, because the players wear form-fitting clothes. (Secularists protested that this would prevent fathers from seeing their daughters' games. The fundamentalist effort failed to pass.) Also, the twenty-two "Islamists" in parliament unanimously opposed the 1993 peace plan for Israel, and demanded eradication of the Jewish nation.

Meanwhile, clandestine guerrillas commit violence in the name of Allah. A group called Prophet Muhammad's Army detonated bombs and set fires in November of 1991. Among their targets were two supermarkets that sold alcohol. Eight of the rebels were sentenced to death for the attacks, but Hussein commuted their sentences to life imprisonment.*

In January 1994, other terrorists assassinated Jordanian diplomat Naeb Maaytah in Lebanon and bombed a theater that showed X-rated movies, injuring seven patrons.

Jordan's leaders openly denounce fundamentalist militancy in the Middle East. "The enemy is religious fanaticism," Crown Prince Hassan bin Talal said in a *New York Times* commentary in May of 1990.

> The real danger lies in an expanding international fundamentalist movement. Jewish extremists constitute one element of this movement. . . . Another element is an Islamic cohort that is influential in the politics of Muslim societies from Southeast Asia westward through Afghanistan to Lebanon and North Africa. Islamic extremists are increasingly active in the *intifada* in the West Bank and Gaza Strip. . . .
>
> Unless peace prevails, there will be a different kind of war to contend with—a war that knows no territorial or national boundaries. . . . The aim of this war would be to reduce national entities to their sectarian components. The only triumphant residue of such a war would be politico-religious fundamentalism—Islamic, Christian, and Jewish. . . . The fanatical war, if unchecked, could extend from Cairo to Islamabad and beyond. We would then witness the ethnic and cultural Lebanonization of our region.

Washington Post Weekly (National Edition), May 25–31, 1992.

Prince Talal said the "domino theory" of Cold War fame now applies to fundamentalism: that country after country might fall to armed zealots. He said Jordan's goal is "to contain the rising tide of religious fananticism."

In elections in November 1993, King Hussein urged Jordanians to reject political zealotry. It worked. Fundamentalists lost six of their seats in parliament, and voters elected a feminist who attacks Muslim male supremacy.

Indonesia

With 180 million people, the island republic of Indonesia is the world's largest Muslim nation. And it ruthlessly devoured one of the world's smallest Catholic nations.

In 1974, the United Nations granted independence to the former Portuguese colony of East Timor, which occupies half an island in the same South Pacific chain as Indonesia. The following year, Indonesia's military forces, armed with U.S. weapons, invaded East Timor, killed an estimated 200,000 of its Catholic people, and annexed it. World leaders and news media hardly noticed.

Sporadic resistance by some Timorese continued in the 1990s. In 1991, a Timorese dissident sought refuge in a Catholic church but was killed by Indonesian soldiers. Two weeks later, thousands of mourners attempted to lay flowers on his grave near Dili, the capital. Indonesian troops opened fire, killing perhaps 200. The atrocity became known because a *New Yorker* magazine reporter was present. He suffered a skull fracture from a rifle butt, yet survived and reported the incident.

In July 1994, Catholic students protested at Dili, saying that Muslim soldiers had trampled the communion wafers during a mass at a Catholic church. Club-swinging troops broke up the protest. Human rights workers said three students were killed and 30 wounded.

Nigeria

In the poor West African nation of Nigeria, northern Muslims and southern Christians have been killing each other periodically in club-and-spear combat for 150 years. Any public religious event by one faith can trigger a riot by the other, usually with burning of churches and mosques.

For example, *Christianity Today* reported that in 1991, government officials issued a permit for German evangelist Reinhard Bonnke to hold a revival in the historic Muslim city of Kano. Bonnke declared that he had "saved" many Muslims, converting them to Jesus. On the eve of the revival, thousands of Muslims marched through Kano and soon turned violent, burning Christian shops and churches. The next day, members of the Christian Ibo tribe counterattacked, destroying Muslim homes, shops, and mosques. The death toll was estimated at 300.

In 1992, in the Muslim-dominated north, religious rioters attacked each other with poisoned spears, rocks, clubs, machetes, knives, and bows and arrows. Outnumbered Christians took refuge in police stations and in a military academy.

Only half of Nigerians can read or write, per capita earnings are about $200 a year, and life expectancy is under fifty years. The nation's dismal conditions are compounded by religious hate.

Bangladesh

A Muslim enclave at the northeast corner of India, Bangladesh suffers conflict between fundamentalists and secularists, mostly on college campuses. In 1993, riots between zealot students and less-religious students caused the closure of thirty universities and colleges. At a medical school in Rajshahi, a gun battle erupted after fundamentalist students beat a secular student who entered a campus mosque.

In the teeming capital of Dhaka, which has a population of 6 million, a newspaper reported that fundamentalist students were being trained with weapons at secret meetings. In retaliation, twenty-five homemade bombs were thrown at the newspaper office, injuring five reporters. Intellectuals in Dhaka demanded a ban on fundamentalist political parties, and called for a national strike to back up their request. Their call had little success.

Meanwhile, a fervent religious group called the Soldiers of Islam offered a $1,250 reward—more than seven times the per capita income in Bangladesh—to anyone who killed a female writer, Taslima Nasrin, whose book, Shame, criticized Muslim attacks on Hindus. The Soldiers of Islam accused her of "blasphemy and conspiracy against Islam." They staged a protest march and called for a national strike if the government didn't arrest the author.

In 1994, Dr. Nasrin was charged with the crime of sacrilege after a newspaper quoted her as saying the Koran's cruel *shariá* code should be revised. Cleric Sayed Islam, leader of the fundamentalist Preachers party, announced that he would pay an additional $2,500 bounty for the author's murder. She, like author Salman Rushdie before her, went into hiding. Almost daily, swarms of religious believers demanded the execution of Dr. Nasrin, the physician-turned-writer. In a mass demonstration, 4,000 angry fundamentalists marched on the parliament in Dhaka to seek her death. They smashed car windshields and headlights. Later, some of them fought a sticks-and-rocks battle with college students who support the author. More than 30 people were injured. Another holy man raised the assassination reward to $5,000, and the violence escalated. Police estimated that 50,000 furious fundamentalists took to the streets in a dozen cities, battling with students and intellectuals supporting the fugitive woman. In one day's clashes, a teen-age boy was killed and 150 people were wounded. Muslim snake-charmers threatened to loose 10,000 deadly cobras in teeming Bangladesh cities if Dr. Nasrin wasn't caught and killed.

The sixteen nations of the European Union offered asylum to the author. Bangladesh's fundamentalists increased their ferment, fighting with secular political groups and university students who backed Dr. Nasrin. In a clash July 26 at the southern port city of Chittagon, six people were killed. On July 29 and 30, another violent rally was held in Dhaka by 50,000 believers who demanded execution of "blasphemers." Rioting with clubs, pipes, and firebombs injured 250 people. Attorney General Aminul Haq said imposing the death penalty for blasphemy would "send us back to the Dark Ages."

After two months in hiding, Dr. Nasrin appeared in a Dhaka court, under heavy police guard, and posted bond on the sacrilege charge. Then she fled to Sweden and went into hiding again, to elude religious assassins. On August 18 she emerged briefly, with armed guards, to accept a prize from a writers group. She told the assembly: "Fundamentalism is spreading darkness in many parts of the world. . . . I have a dream, a dream of a world . . . where fundamentalist insanity would be unknown."

Bangladesh's rural Muslim *mullahs* sometimes attack welfare workers who teach girls to read, who instruct women on birth-control methods, and who teach families how to avoid disease. In 1994, at the town of Haripur, five clerics beat Abdur Rashid, a field worker for Friends of Village Development, because he had ignored their commands to stop educating women. They clubbed him to the ground with shoes, forced his father to shave the son's head, and fined the father $625 (the equivalent of two years' income).

News reports said religious zealots burned 55 girls classrooms in Bangladesh in 1994 and vandalized 1,300 others.

Trinidad

The tropical Caribbean island of Trinidad has an odd religious mix: one-third of its people are Catholic, nearly another third are Protestant, one-fourth are Hindu, and only 6 percent are Muslim. Yet fanatics among the Muslim minority staged a brief military coup in 1990.

Apparently armed secretly by Libya, a group called *Jamaat al-Muslimeen* (the Muslim Group) attacked the national television station and the parliament building. They took forty-seven government officials hostage, including Prime Minister Arthur Robinson, who was shot in both legs and tied to a chair wired with explosives. Two dozen people were killed in the takeover. Several police officers died when the Muslims rammed a bomb-rigged vehicle into their headquarters. Bodies lay in streets, unreachable because of sniper fire. Fire destroyed part of the capital, Port-of-Spain.

The Muslim leader, Yasin Abu-Bakr, a former policeman, talked with radio reporters. As for the people killed in the coup, he said: "Whatever blood there is has cleansed us." Asked about his connection to Libya, he said: "We are Muslim. Libyans are Muslim. . . . We have received mutual aid."*

Five days later, the Muslims abruptly released their hostages and surrendered. Abu-Bakr bowed to Mecca and told reporters: "Let God be praised, let God be praised." Prime Minister Robinson, who had promised the rebels

---

*The Associated Press, July 29, 1990.

amnesty if they laid down their weapons, immediately jailed them on murder and treason charges. Two years later, however, courts ruled that the amnesty pledge must be honored, and the Muslims were freed.

Libya

Libya also inflicts the harsh *shariá* religious law. In 1994, leader Muammar Qaddafi decreed that anyone engaging in business without a license will be "considered a thief in accordance with the *shariá*. His hand will be cut off." He outlined this new policy to leaders of Libya's "purification committees." According to a *New York Times* report in June of 1994 about Amnesty International, the committees were created after Libya passed "purification laws" in February to enforce the Islamic punishments of amputations and floggings.

Iraq

Iraq likewise promulgated the *shariá* in 1994. Newswire stories reported that Saddam Hussein decreed that first-time thieves would have their right hands chopped off, and slow-learners who commit a second offense would lose their left foot. Later, he expanded the decree to say that farmers refusing to sell grain to the government would suffer amputation of hands.

Cyprus

A volatile mix of religion, politics, nationalism, and terrorism has kept U.N. peacekeepers busy in Cyprus for three decades, preventing the island's Muslim Turks and Christian Greeks from killing each other.

During the Crusades, the Mediterranean island was conquered by Richard the Lionhearted and given to the king of the new Christian realm established in Jerusalem. It has been a battle zone ever since.

After World War I, Britain seized Cyprus as a colony. Greek-speaking Christians on the island sought union with Greece. The Turkish-speaking Muslim minority objected. After World War II, Archbishop Makarios took up the Christian cause. He was exiled, and terrorism broke out. Finally, in 1960, Cyprus was granted independence, with the returned Makarios as president and a Muslim as vice president.

Christian-Muslim coexistence lasted only three years. Then fighting spread across the island. Muslims in the south fled for safety to the north, where most Muslims lived. Christians in the north did the opposite. The United Nations rushed in a peacekeeping force to maintain a ceasefire. Although the gunfire ceased, hostility didn't.

In 1974, Christian militants seeking union with Greece overthrew President Makarios, whereupon Turkey invaded the island to protect its Muslims. Still more Christians fled to the south as refugees. The northern third of Cyprus was declared a separate Muslim nation, but only Turkey recognized it.

In the 1990s, little has changed on the hate-divided island. United Nations troops still are required to serve as a buffer.

A British writer noted sardonically that, despite their estrangement, the Muslim men and Christian men of Cyprus agree in one respect: both subjugate women and demand that brides be virgins, lest male honor be sullied.

Pakistan

The Indus Valley, in the heart of Pakistan, contains relics of one of the oldest known civilizations, dating back 5,000 years. Judging by religious cruelty of the 1990s, the region has made little progress in five millennia.

The government of Pakistan, a Muslim nation, decreed in 1991 that anyone commiting blasphemy by insulting the Prophet Muhammad must be hanged. It also decreed that unmarried lovers may be stoned to death, and that other offenders may have their hands or feet chopped off, or be flogged, under the *shariá* code of the Koran.

Among the first victims of the new laws were two American brothers who had converted to Islam and moved to Pakistan. Convicted of robbing a bank, each was sentenced to have his right hand and left foot chopped off. At their trial, the brothers insisted they were innocent, and one called the Islamic judges "a court of infidels." Soon afterward, Pakistan's Supreme Court ruled that the brothers were innocent, and freed them. They shouted to reporters, *Allahu akbar!* ("God is great").

Occasionally, conflict erupts between Sunni and Shi'ite Muslims in Pakistan. In 1990, at the city of Shujaabad, 200 miles south of the eastern city of Lahore, youths from a Shi'ite group threw grenades at a Sunni religious procession, killing seven people and wounding 79.

Shi'ite-Sunni attacks resumed in Pakistan in 1994. On July 12, according to Associated Press reports, two Sunni boys praying in a mosque at the eastern city of Lahore were killed by a grenade, presumably tossed by militant Shi'ites. Their deaths caused Prime Minister Benazir Bhutto to warn an assembly of judges and lawyers: "The demon of sectarianism could threaten the very existence of this country." On July 23, a busload of Shi'ites returning from a mosque in the southern port city of Karachi was attacked by gunmen riding on three motorcycles and carrying automatic weapons. Six Shi'ites were killed and 25 were wounded. A militant Shi'ite leader blamed Sunnis for the massacre and vowed retaliation. The following day, in Karachi, gunmen attacked three Shi'ite mosques, killing three people and injuring 13, including six children hurt by a bomb while they studied the Koran.

Pakistan's six million Christians sometimes are targets of similar violence. In Lahore in 1994, four Christians were taken to court on charges of insulting Islam by writing graffiti on a mosque. As the four left the courthouse, Muslim gunmen opened fire, killing one and wounding the other three. The assassins fled and vanished.

Women are subjugated in Pakistan, as in most Muslim nations. In 1994, a report documented hundreds of cases of men throwing acid in the faces of young women who spurned their offers of marriage. Also in 1994, at a village south of Islamabad, police charged a doctor with setting fire to the sacred Koran, a blasphemous crime punishable by death. Before he could be tried, an enraged mob dragged him from the police station, doused him with kerosene, and burned him alive.

Pakistan was headquarters of the world's most religious banking empire, the Bank of Commerce and Credit International (BCCI). Founder Agha Abedi expanded BCCI into a worldwide institution, telling employees they served "the Almighty" in furtherance of "a divine goal." His staff was required to abstain from liquor, tobacco, and gambling. Prayer rooms were built in branch offices. But BCCI secretly was a cesspool of corruption, linked to bribery, drug smuggling, embezzlement, gun-running, and terrorism. Prostitutes were provided to important clients. Billions of dollars were looted from accounts. New York District Attorney Robert Morgenthau accused the institution of perpetrating "the largest bank fraud in world financial history." In 1994, a dozen BCCI executives were convicted in the United Arab Emirates and sentenced to long prison terms. Abedi drew eight years, but was hiding in Pakistan, which refused to extradite him.

Many Pakistanis aren't fundamentalists. In 1993, voters chose liberal Benazir Bhutto as prime minister for a second time, ignoring clerics who said Islam forbids a woman to lead. A few holy men issued *fatwas* mandating her murder, but no zealots tried it. The situation turned uglier in 1994 when her justice minister, Iqbal Haider, proposed revising blasphemy laws to prevent filing of false

179

charges against Christians and members of the outlawed Ahmedi sect. Cleric Abdulla Darkhwasti branded Haider an infidel and offered $40,000 to any believer who killed him. If an assassin died in the attempt, Darkhwasti said, he would go instantly to paradise as a Muslim martyr.

Meanwhile, bumper stickers appeared in Lahore exhorting true Muslims to kill Bhutto's family-planning minister and two other government members.

Kuwait

Islam's double standard in sexual rules for men and women is visible in the lifestyle of Sheik Jaber al-Sabah, the ruling emir of Kuwait. After American-led forces in the Persian Gulf War in 1991 restored the Sabah family to power, the *New York Times* reported: "At regular intervals— sometimes weekly—Sheik Jaber is said to marry a young virgin on Thursday night, the eve of the Islamic sabbath, only to divorce on Friday." The Koran permits a man as many as four wives ("or what your right hands possess," an allowance that traditionally authorized concubines). To divorce, a man need only declare that he is repudiating a wife.

Soviet Disunion

The collapse of communism spurred Islamic flareups in several southern republics of the former Soviet Union.

The most violent was in Tajikistan, a mountain enclave north of Afghanistan and Pakistan. In 1990, Tajik Muslim extremists mobbed buses and attacked girls whose heads weren't covered. They demanded that the government halt sales of pork. The street protests turned into armed clashes between religious militants and police, with numerous deaths. Russian army units were sent to suppress the uprising.

In 1991, Tajikistan established an independent government. Soon, fundamentalists and other dissidents rebelled. In 1992, the Muslim-led forces temporarily seized the capital and took power, but they were routed by government troops. Russia sent more units to put down the uprising and prevent religious war from sweeping other southern republics. The Tajik insurgents were driven south, across the border into Afghanistan. The fighting killed 20,000 people and drove 500,000 from their homes. Skirmishes along the border continued in 1994.

Other Muslim upheavals arose sporadically in other regions. As if the struggling new Russian government didn't have enough religious problems, a Ukrainian female cult leader who claims to be God told thousands of followers that the world would end in November 1993. It didn't, and she and her aides were jailed for scuffling with police.

Lebanon

Humanity has a very short memory. International horrors are soon forgotten as new ones rivet the public's attention.

181

Already the religious civil war that ravaged lovely Lebanon through the 1980s and killed 150,000 of its people has vanished from newspaper commentaries and television analyses.

Actually, it was merely the latest time that religious tribalism has produced war in Lebanon. Fifteen centuries ago, Maronite Christians, who disagreed with Byzantine ecclesiastics about the divine will of Jesus, were persecuted and driven into mountains at the eastern end of the Mediterranean Sea. Then a Muslim *jihad* conquered the region in the 600s. Then a Christian uprising against the Muslims was crushed in the 700s. This was followed by attacks by dissident Shi'ite Muslims, who seized a stronghold at the turn of the millennium. Christian Crusaders conquered Lebanon in 1099, followed by Muslim Turks, who conquered in 1516. A ruling Turkish family converted to Christianity in the 1700s. An uprising by the Druses, a splinter Shi'ite sect, toppled the Christians in 1842. This bloodshed was followed by a gory civil war between Shi'ites, Sunnis, Druses, and Maronites, which wracked Lebanon in the 1850s.

After World War I, France acquired Lebanon as a colony and suppressed hostility between the sects. In 1946, France freed the nation, which was to rule itself by power-sharing: a Maronite Christian always would be president, a Sunni Muslim would be premier, a Shi'ite would be speaker of parliament, and legislative seats would be allocated to religious groups according to their population strength.

The arrangement worked until the 1970s, when poor Shi'ites rioted against privileged Christians, and civil war broke out. Palestinian refugees from Israel joined the Muslim side. Soon ten different religious militias were in combat, some forming alliances, then turning on each other. Christian and Muslim sectors in the capital, Beirut, were separated by a "Green Line"—a free-fire zone for snipers of both faiths. Car bomb explosions, ambushes and assassinations occurred daily. By 1990, the international organization UNICEF estimated that 40,000 Lebanese children had been killed, more had been maimed, and still more had been orphaned.

In 1989, the Arab League negotiated a peace plan, but a renegade Christian general rebelled against it, prolonging the war until his militia was crushed in late 1990. By then, the beautiful coastal nation and its capital, once considered "the Paris of the Middle East," were in ruins, and survivors were wracked by poverty. Nearly 100,000 buildings were destroyed in the war, sewage treatment plants were beyond repair, telephone systems were disabled, and other extensive damage to the infrastructure remained.

Joblessness and deprivation in the war's wake bred an ominous rise of Shi'ite fundamentalism among the poor. Car bombings and assassinations became more numerous in the 1990s. Militants were recruited by the *Hezbollah* militia that prowls southern Lebanon, fighting border skirmishes with Israelis. Leaders who attempted to rebuild Lebanon tried to suppress the unrest.

On February 27, 1994, two days after the Hebron mosque massacre, a bomb exploded in a Maronite Christian church just north of Beirut. Nine Christians were killed and 60 were wounded. Not long thereafter, a bomb killed three at a Christian political party headquarters; a bomb wrapped as a Teacher's Day gift was delivered to a Christian teacher; and a time bomb was found in a Christian school, set to explode while children were in class.

Muslim militants were suspected of these attacks, but authorities accused an extremist Christian party of the church bombing. In a raid on one of the Christian group's offices, police found 300 assault rifles, 20 rocket-propelled grenade launchers, 20 machine guns and 3 truckloads of ammunition, all kept in violation of the disarmament that followed the 1980s civil war. The group's leader, Samir Geagea, later was charged with murder in the church bombing. A magistrate accused him of plotting "to establish a Christian mini-state" in Lebanon.

Also in 1994, Lebanon's chief Shi'ite cleric, Sheik Mohammed Shamdseddine, urged Shi'ite farmers to resume growing hashish for the world narcotics market because a United Nations program failed to find new jobs for growers.

Throughout the Muslim world, religion is grim and inescapable. When the Ayatollah Khomeini called for the holy murder of author Salman Rushdie, travel writer Paul Theroux said in the February 13, 1992, *New York Times* op-ed page that his first impulse was to laugh, as if it were "a very bad joke, a bit like 'Papa Doc' Duvalier putting a voodoo curse on Graham Greene for writing *The Comedians.*"

"Of course," he wrote, "I did not foresee much merriment about *The Satanic Verses* in any Islamic state, where building blueprints have to be subjected to a board of Islamic scholars, the *ulema,* so the authorities can make sure that no toilet faces Mecca. Where toys and calendars and mugs based on the Muppet figure of 'Miss Piggy' are dragged from shops by the religious police and ritually destroyed. Where there are equally batty and murderous *fatwas,* such as the recent one delivered by a Saudi Arabian official cleric who declared that all Shi'ite Muslims are heretics and should be killed. You know you have traveled through the looking glass when you are in a land where Miss Piggy is seen as the very embodiment of evil."

14

The United States

The United States doesn't suffer religious warfare, yet isolated, localized horrors of faith occur by the hundreds. They happen week after week, in many varieties, usually drawing only brief notice in news reports.

For example, Florida holy man Yahweh ben Yahweh (alias Hulon Mitchell, Jr.) and six leaders of his Temple of Love were convicted in 1992 of murdering 14 church defectors and others. The misnamed sect is a puritanical, Old Testament-style African-American group with perhaps 10,000 members. Yahweh taught his disciples to hate "white devils." To attain the inner circle, believers had to kill a white person for Yahweh. (Federal prosecutors proved seven such murders.) Lieutenants became "death angels" assigned to kill church backsliders and slum residents who resisted the temple's efforts to take over poor apartment complexes. Some victims were decapitated. Others' ears were cut off and brought to Yahweh as souvenirs. Yahweh was sentenced to eighteen years in prison, and his six disciples drew from fifteen to sixteen years each.

A completely different American church horror is fundamentalist violence against abortion clinics, which escalated to murder in 1993. As born-again pickets surrounded a clinic in Pensacola, Florida, one of them, Michael Griffin, drew a pistol and shot the clinic physician, Dr. David Gunn, three times in the back. The previous Sunday, Griffin had attended a Pensacola Assemby of God church, whose members speak in "the unknown tongue." Griffin asked the congregation to "pray that Dr. Gunn would receive Jesus Christ as his savior and stop killing children." After the murder, a fundamentalist magazine called Griffin a "hero," but he was convicted in 1994 and sentenced to life imprisonment.

Not long after the Pensacola murder, a devout Oregon woman, Shelly Shannon, took similar action at a Wichita clinic. She fired several shots at Dr. George Tiller, wounding him in both arms. Later, she boasted to fellow believers: "It was the most holy, the most righteous thing I've ever done." She was convicted of attempted murder and was sentenced to eleven years in prison. According to the court transcript, when the judge told her she had done wrong, she replied: "They said that about Jesus." She added that she would "always be obedient to God, no matter what it costs." Meanwhile, a Catholic priest, the Rev. David Trosch, attempted to place newspaper advertisements calling it "justifiable homicide" for Christians to kill abortion doctors.

In May of 1994, the fanatics suffered two setbacks: Congress made it a federal crime to blockade an abortion clinic. And a Texas jury returned a $1 million damage judgment against various fundamentalists, such as members of the Lambs of Christ, who mobbed a Houston clinic during the 1992 Republican National Convention. In June the U.S. Supreme Court upheld a Florida lower court decision preventing protesters from blocking abortion clinics. But court rulings couldn't deter the fundamentalist fury. On July 29, three people were blasted by a shotgun as they arrived at a different Pensacola clinic. The clinic physician, Dr. John Britton, was wearing a bulletproof vest, but died of head wounds. He had been escorted by a retired couple, James and June Barrett. The husband was killed, and the wife suffered an arm wound. A fanatical minister who often had advocated clinic violence was charged with murder. Thus, zealots who call themselves "pro-life" came to symbolize brutal death.

Another type of church horror in the United States is the pederasty scandal devastating the Catholic Church. About 400 priests are known to have molested children under their care, and scores have been sentenced to prison. One priest, the Rev. James Porter, sodomized perhaps 100 children in three states, including a boy in a full body cast who couldn't move to resist. Porter was convicted in 1993 and drew eighteen years in prison.

Some other convictions: The Rev. John R. Hanlon of Massachusetts received three life sentences in April 1994 for raping an altar boy. The same month, the Rev. Edward Pipala of Goshen, New York, was sentenced to eight years for taking 11 boys across state lines for sex. The Rev. Earl Bierman of Kentucky drew a twenty-year sentence in July 1993 for extensive child-molesting. The Rev. Robert E. Mayer of Chicago got a three-year term in early 1993 for abusing a thirteen-year-old girl. The Rev. Andrew Andersen of California began serving a six-year term in 1990 on 26 counts of molesting altar boys.

Damage suits have cost American Catholics as much as $500 million, according to some estimates. In late 1993, the Servants of the Paraclete Treatment Center in New Mexico agreed to pay $8 million to 25 plaintiffs who had been sodomized by Father Porter, and the Archdiocese of Santa Fe agreed to a $13 million settlement with 30 plaintiffs molested by the Rev. Jason Sigler. A jury in Arkansas awarded $1.5 million to a young woman who alleged that the Rev. Timothy Sugrue molested her when she was eight years old. In April 1994, a Pennsylvania jury found the Altoona-Johnstown Diocese liable for $1.6 million in damages to a young man who was molested by the Rev. Francis E. Luddy. A young Minnesota man won a $3.5 million judgment for abuse by the Rev. Thomas Adamson, but it was reduced to $1 million on appeal. Hundreds of other cases, criminal and civil, were making their way through courts. Renowned priest, sociologist, and novelist Andrew Greeley estimated that from 2,000 to 4,000 pedophile priests in the United States have molested more than 100,000 children, "each one a human being who has suffered a terrible personal tragedy at the hands of a slayer of the soul."

But Catholicism isn't the only faith tainted by lurid

crimes. Multitudes of cases involving Protestants also occur, drawing less attention. Here are some items from the news wires:

Pentecostal evangelist Mario Leyva of Columbus, Georgia, who railed against "filth" and "smut," furtively sodomized more than 100 church boys. He was caught, and began serving a twenty-year prison term in 1990. Two assistant pastors got fifteen and twelve years for transporting the boys across state lines for orgies.

*   *   *

The Rev. Roy Yanke of Beverly Hills, Michigan, pleaded guilty in 1991 to robbing fourteen banks of $47,000 to pay for his daily use of prostitutes. He got seven years in prison.

*   *   *

Televangelist William Wasmus of Columbus, Ohio, was sentenced to 104 years in prison in 1994 for child pornography and engaging in sex with children. He used the video equipment of his Church of the Living Savior to make "kiddie porn."

*   *   *

Television minister Jim Bakker, who was sentenced to forty-five years in prison for swindling 145,000 donors to his PTL (Praise the Lord) Club, was ordered in 1990 to repay $130 million to the unlucky believers. But they got nothing, because Bakker was in a cell, his religious empire gone. Bakker's sentence was later reduced, and he is now in a halfway house.

*   *   *

Born-again con artist Michael Douglas of Antioch, Illinois, who specialized in investments for rich fundamentalists, was sentenced to twelve years in prison in 1991 for swindling 131 people out of $31 million.

*   *   *

Army chaplain aide Steven Ritchie of Fort Lewis, Washington, was sentenced to twenty-six years in prison in 1990 for raping a six-week-old baby girl.

*   *   *

Radio evangelist Willie Winters of Kalamazoo, Michigan, already serving two life terms for a shooting spree, was indicted again in 1992 on charges of killing his brother-in-law for $22,000 in insurance money. He was convicted of both murder and mail fraud in the insurance scheme, and received yet another life sentence.

*   *   *

The Rev. Jerry Wilson of Monticello, Indiana, who said his preaching came "from God Himself," had an affair with his secretary at the Bible Tabernacle Church and planted a bomb to kill her husband. In 1992, Wilson was sentenced to 108 years in prison.

* * *

Religious zealot Reynaldo Gonzales began raging about Bible prophecies on a Greyhound bus in Phoenix, Arizona, in 1992. He forced the driver to take him and other passengers on a 300-mile dash across the West, reaching speeds of 80 miles an hour, to his home at Colton, California. Emerging from the bus, he attacked police officers in his driveway and was shot to death.

* * *

Evangelist Don McCary of Chattanooga, Tennessee, drew a seventy-two-year prison sentence in 1992 for sodomizing four boys. His twin brother, Christian comedian Ron McCary, is in prison for raping a six-year-old boy. Their older brother, the Rev. Richard McCary, previously was imprisoned for child-molesting. He served time in a California prison in the 1980s, then was returned to prison in the 1990s for another abuse.

* * *

Lutheran youth worker James Allen Weller of Redwood City, California, received a forty-eight-year sentence in 1991 for molesting children, some of whom were only ten years old.

*   *   *

Fountain of Life evangelist Jim Whittington of Greenville, North Carolina, was indicted in 1992 on charges of swindling a paraplegic woman out of $900,000. He called the federal charge an attack "on the gospel of the Lord Jesus Christ." Nonetheless a federal jury found Whittington guilty of eleven counts of fraud.

*   *   *

Church deacon Henry Meinholz, fifty-three, of Kingston, Massachusetts, was convicted in 1991 of raping and suffocating a thirteen-year-old girl. He was sentenced to life in prison.

*   *   *

The Rev. Lloyd Davis, fifty-seven, of First Christian Fellowship in Waukegan, Illinois, was sentenced to thirty-one years in prison for child pornography and sexual abuse of teen-age boys.

*   *   *

A woman evangelist, Mary Nicholson of Pace, Florida, was charged in 1990 with telling a mother to beat her baby daughter in order to drive out "six demons." The mother pleaded guilty to pummeling the infant to death. The evangelist was convicted of first degree murder and sentenced to life in prison.

*   *   *

The Rev. Virgil Carpenter, forty-eight, of Bible Missionary Church in Ontario, Oregon, was convicted of sodomizing a nine-year-old girl over a period of more than a year. He told his followers not to worry because "I'm right with the Lord."

*   *   *

Self-proclaimed prophet Gilbert Michaels of southern California was charged in 1992 with committing bank robberies to get money to build an impregnable bunker in which he planned to survive the coming Battle of Armageddon. According to a late February 1994 *Los Angeles Times* story, a companion who helped the prophet rob the banks subsequently was sentenced to thirty years in prison, but a judge decided that Michaels was insane and shelved his case.

*   *   *

Presbyterian minister Bruce Brigden, fifty-seven, of Alva, Oklahoma, got forty years in prison for molesting eleven girls, some only four years of age. He was later stabbed to death by fellow prison inmates.

*   *   *

A religious dentist, Dr. David Johns, stabbed his wife to death in 1993, slashed himself with the knife, and ran naked down a street of Indiana, Pennsylvania, chanting Bible verses. He told police he was Jesus. Pointing to his wounds, he said "I am resurrected." At his trial in 1994, he pleaded insanity, but was convicted and sentenced to spend his life either in prison or in a secure mental hospital.

*   *   *

The Rev. Richard Jones of the Family Life Church at Park Hills, Missouri, was sentenced to 189 years in prison in 1994 for sexually abusing children. Boys testified that Jones told them his sexual acts were "sanctioned by the Bible."

*   *   *

One of several children molested by youth minister Keith Geren of Wayside Baptist Church in Miami, Florida, was awarded $6.7 million in damages by a jury in early 1994.

*   *   *

The Rev. Duane Smith, operator of a fundamentalist school in Laporte, Indiana, was sentenced to twelve years in prison in 1992 for molesting his pupils.

*   *   *

. TV evangelist Robert Tilton of Dallas, Texas, was found liable for $1.5 million in damages in April 1994 on grounds that he had bilked a Florida couple out of $3,500 in donations.

*   *   *

Michael Turner, a Catholic living in Annapolis, Maryland, pleaded guilty in July 1994 to beating his mother to death with a small statue of the Virgin Mary.

*   *   *

Mormon Sunday school teacher John Midgett of California was sentenced to thirty years in prison for molesting eight girls, some only five years of age.

*   *   *

The Rev. Jon Walker of Springfield Baptist Church in California drew thirteen years in prison for sexually misusing a thirteen-year-old girl. When his parishioners pleaded for leniency, a prosecutor said their support was "sad testimony to the fact that Mr. Walker's life has been a fraud."

The Rev. James Randazzo, founder of the Spiral of Friends Church at Molina, Colorado, was convicted in 1989 of ten counts of drug use and molesting children. He fled the country, but was caught in Hungary in 1992 and brought back for sentencing. He drew a sixteen-year prison term.

*   *   *

The Nation of Islam, a controversial Black Muslim church whose leaders need armed bodyguards, suffered violence again in 1994. Minister Khallid Muhammad gave a speech in a University of California auditorium where security was so strict that listeners were searched repeatedly for guns. But as Muhammad left the auditorium, he, four bodyguards, and a bystander were wounded by a defrocked minister. Muhammad's followers beat the gunman savagely and would have killed him had police not intervened.

The Nation of Islam's most famous assassination happened two decades earlier, when dissident minister Malcolm X was killed in church by twenty-one shots fired by three Nation of Islam members.

*   *   *

Followers of the late guru Bhagwan Sri Rajneesh still were being prosecuted in the 1990s. The guru's sex-saturated Oregon commune collapsed in the 1980s after Rajneesh and female aides were charged with various crimes. His chief assistant, Ma Anand Sheela, who carried a .357 magnum, pleaded guilty to attempted murder, arson, immigration fraud, and poisoning 750 residents of an Oregon town by slipping salmonella bacteria into restaurant salad bars. In 1990, one of the guru's former female aides, Ma Dyan Yogini, pleaded guilty to conspiracy to murder a federal prosecutor, and was sentenced to two years in prison.

The United States even had a human sacrifice case in the 1990s. Ohioan Jeffrey Lundgren had been a Mormon minister until he was defrocked in 1988 for psychotic behavior. Afterward, he led a band of followers at a farm thirty miles east of Cleveland, and used several women as sex slaves. Planning to move the band to Missouri, Lundgren confided to other leaders that God wanted a sacrificial "cleansing" to bring a blessing on the move. A member family was chosen. One by one, the father, mother, and three daughters were lured into the cult barn, bound with tape, then shot and buried. The sacrifice was performed in April 1989, but remained a secret for nine months. In January 1990, acting on a tip from a defector, Ohio police dug under the barn and found the decomposed bodies. By then, the cultists had moved, first to West Virginia, then Missouri, then California. All the cult leaders were caught and drew long prison terms, except for Lundgren, who was sentenced to death.

A Hare Krishna commune and "golden temple" in West Virginia made murder headlines in the 1990s. The temple's spiritual leader, Kirtanananda Swami Bhaktipada (alias Keith Ham, a Baptist preacher's son), was convicted in 1991 of arranging the death of a dissident member, whose body was found buried in a creek. The swami got thirty years in prison, but told his worshipers: "God is in control and he does everything perfectly for his purpose." Another commune leader, Thomas Drescher, was convicted of killing a second dissident on a Los Angeles street. Prosecutors said Swami Bhaktipada paid Drescher $8,000 for the murder. The swami's conviction later was reversed on grounds that testimony about child molestation and homosexuality in the commune had prejudiced the jury.

As for religious tribalism, the United States has various forms of it. Believers tend to stick to their own kind; the more fervent their beliefs, the more they become a subculture at odds with the mainstream of society. Fundamentalists in the United States, like their counterparts in Muslim lands, are puritans who want to impose their strictures on worldly people around them. I see it constantly in my work as editor of a newspaper in the Appalachian "Bible Belt." Hidebound mountain Protestants clamor for narrow goals: they want the death penalty restored, sexy movies and magazines banned, worship imposed in public schools by the power of government, abortion outlawed, and sex education limited to lectures on abstinence.

Fundamentalist activism easily can breed violence. I witnessed it firsthand some years ago in a famous West

Virginia episode—a war against "godless textbooks." It featured mob ferment, school bombings, two shootings, a coal strike, federal convictions, and international notoriety.

During this nightmare, Charleston acquired an image somewhat like Dayton, Tennessee, home of the Scopes trial, the 1925 clash over evolution. Ironically, the whole insurrection was pointless, because the school books were just routine texts. Their sins existed only in the fevered imagination of the zealots.

The upheaval was rooted in the period when religious conservatives rebelled against liberal excesses of the 1960s. The first to jump into the limelight was the Rev. Charles Meadows, who went before the West Virginia Legislature in February of 1969 to demand a return of the death penalty. He testified that he would "be glad to pull the switch myself" at executions. Then he attacked sex education in Kanawha County schools. He rented the Charleston Civic Center theater and invited "Bible-believing Christians" to a rally against the "pornography" of sex education. Committees were formed and a movement grew.

Alice Moore, wife of a Church of Christ pastor, became the movement's candidate for the school board in 1970. She said sex education was part of a "humanistic, atheistic attack on God." Church groups poured money into her campaign. She won and became the board's ayatollah, supporting Bibles for students and expulsion of pregnant girls.

Moore's moralizing had minor effect until 1974, when new textbooks were up for adoption. She denounced the books as irreligious, and a protest grew. A group of twenty-seven born-again clergymen called the texts "immoral and indecent." (Rascals like me hunted for the indecencies in the books, but found only ordinary school topics.)

On the night of the adoption vote, 1,000 protesters surrounded the school board office. Despite this menace, members voted three to two in favor of the books. Afterward, a group called Christian American Parents picketed a discount store chain because the chain's president, a board member, had voted yes.

When school opened, evangelists urged "true Christians" to keep their children home. Attendance fell 20 percent, more so in the poor end of the county. The Rev. Marvin Horan led a rally of 2,000 protesters. Mobs surrounded schools and blockaded school bus garages. Teachers were threatened. So were families who didn't join the boycott.

About 3,500 coal miners went on strike against the texts, and picketed industries. Flying rocks, screams, and danger were constant. Frightened people in some communities carried pistols. Having halted many school buses, the textbook pickets stopped city buses, leaving 11,000 low-income people without transportation.

When pickets surrounded a truck terminal, a janitor fired a shot wounding one. Other picketers beat the janitor savagely. The next day, an armed man who panicked when pickets surged toward him, fired a shot that wounded a bystander. Two book protesters were jailed for smashing windshields.

The school board secured a court injunction against disrupters, but it didn't help. Finally the superintendent closed the schools, saying the safety of the children couldn't be guaranteed. Schools also closed in adjoining counties.

Network TV crews swarmed to Charleston. A cameraman was trounced by fundamentalists at a rally. The Rev. Ezra Graley led a march on the state Capitol and filed a federal suit against the textbooks. Graley and other ministers were jailed for contempt of the court injunction.

The schools eventually reopened even though the boycott resumed. Some pro-boycott ministers prayed for God to kill the board members who endorsed the books. A grade school was hit by a Molotov cocktail. Five shots hit a school bus. A dynamite blast damaged another grade school. A bigger blast damaged the school central office.

Near-riot conditions continued. Robert Dornan of California, a pornography foe who was later elected to Congress, addressed a crowd of 3,000. Protesters started "born-again" schools. A fundamentalist politician actually tried to make eastern Kanawha, the heart of the protest, a separate county.

Minister Horan and three of his followers were indicted for the bombings. Ku Klux Klan leaders led a Charleston rally to support them. An imperial wizard from Georgia said the Kanawha textbooks contained "the most vulgar, vile, and filthy words in print," which was odd, since nonfundamentalists couldn't find any obscenities in them.

During the trial in 1975, other followers said Horan had led the dynamite plot, telling them there was "a time to kill." They said the plotters talked of wiring dynamite caps into the gas tanks of cars in which families were driving their children to school during the boycott. All four defendants went to federal prison.

Horan's conviction ended the protest, while other leaders lost face. Minister Meadows left his church after admitting involvement with a female religion teacher. Minister Graley's wife left him and he sued to recover the luxury car she took. School board member Moore abruptly left the state.

Looking back, it was a season of madness, a frenzy over nothing, like a famous ferment among U.S. fundamentalists who thought the moon-and-stars logo on Procter & Gamble soap was a secret sign of Satan. The Kanawha chaos showed how zealots can turn trivia into tragedy. It gave insight into the kind of psychological forces that impel holy wars in India and elsewhere.

*   *   *

For many years, I was the *Charleston Gazette*'s religion reporter, and it gave me the opportunity to take a close look at people who believe simplistically in magical faiths. They are easy prey for charlatans, oddballs, and psychopaths. Any criticism of their leaders is seen as the work of Satan. Here are some Bible Belt episodes I covered:

Clarence "Tiz" Jones was a beloved evangelist, whose supporters refused to see that he also was a burglar. He had been a West Virginia champion amateur boxer in his youth, but succumbed to liquor and evil companions, and spent a hitch in state prison. Then he was converted and became a popular Nazarene revivalist. He roamed the state, drawing big crowds, with many in the audience coming forward to be saved.

But police noticed a pattern: In towns where Jones preached, burglaries happened. Eventually, officers charged him with a break-in. This caused a backlash among churches. Followers said Satan and His agents were framing the preacher. A "Justice for Tiz Jones" committee raised a defense fund. Protest marches were held. Later, Jones was nabbed red-handed in another burglary, and his guilt was clear. He went back to prison.

Another spectacular mountain minister was "Dr." Paul Collett, a faith-healer who claimed he could resurrect the dead—if they hadn't yet been embalmed. Collett set up a big tent in Charleston and drew multitudes, including many in wheelchairs and on crutches. The healer said he had revived a corpse during a previous stop. He urged believers to bring him bodies of loved ones—before embalming.

Collett moved his show into an old movie house and started broadcasting over radio stations. One night he said a cancer fell onto the stage. Another night he said he turned water into wine.

I attended a service and wrote a skeptical newspaper account, focusing on his many money collections. After the article appeared, forty of Collett's followers invaded the paper's newsroom. Luckily, it was my day off. The night city editor called the police, and also summoned burly printers, who backed the throng out the door.

Collett claimed to have 10,000 adherents. For five

years he collected money to build a twelve-doored Bible Church of All Nations, which was to be "the biggest tabernacle in West Virginia." Then he moved to Canada, leaving not a rack behind.

He returned some years later and preached at a serpent-handling church in a rural hollow. I often wrote about the ardent mountain worshipers who pick up buzzing rattlesnakes and thrust their hands into fire to show their faith. They're earnest and simple people, even though they have a high mortality rate during prayer services.

The leader of the serpent church, Elzie Preast, who never took money from members, began to suspect that Dr. Collett was bilking his congregation. In an Old Testament-type showdown, the two ministers scuffled, one shouting "Manifest him, Lord!" and the other yelling "Rebuke the devil!"

A former University of Charleston sociologist, Dr. Nathan Gerrard, studied the serpent phenomenon. He administered a psychological test to members of a flock, and then gave the same test to a nearby Methodist congregation as a control group. The serpent-handlers came out mentally healthier.

Once the great Harvard theologian Harvey Cox accompanied Dr. Gerrard and me to a serpent church. When the worshipers began their trance-like "dancing in the spirit," we were surprised to see Dr. Cox leap up and join the hoofing.

Later, visiting professors accompanied us to another serpent church. One professor's wife, barely five feet tall, was an opera soprano. The worshipers—whose music usually is the twang of electric guitars—asked her to sing. She stood on the altar rail and trilled an aria from *La Boheme* while the congregation listened respectfully.

Colorful evangelists of many types abound in Appalachia. One I knew was faith-healer Henry Lacy, who handed out calling cards saying simply "Lacy the Stranger." He often came into our newsroom to lay hands on reporters to cure their hangovers. He once offered to halt a cold wave in West Virginia if state officials would return his confiscated driver's license.

And there was roving healer A. A. Allen, who toured with jars containing bodies that he said were demons he had cast out of the sick. (Skeptics said they were frogs.) Allen vanished after a revival in Wheeling, and was found dead of alcoholism in a San Francisco hotel room.

(Marjoe Gortner, the boy evangelist who later confessed that his show was a fraud, said Allen once advised him how to tell when a revival was finished and it was time to go to the next city: "When you can turn people on their head and shake them and no money falls out, then you know God's saying, 'Move on, son.' ")

Fundamentalism of this sort can be viewed as a carnival, even a comedy—yet there's an ugly side. Many low-income believers give their money to ministers who secretly are criminal or psychotic. The truth doesn't emerge until prosecutions occur.

The most horrifying religious evils occur in cults living apart from American society. An infamous example was the Jonestown commune led by California minister Jim Jones. More than 900 of his followers took cyanide and gave it to their children in a 1978 mass suicide that shocked the world.

Another notorious group was the Church of the First Born of the Lamb of God, which wreaked havoc in Utah and Mexico in the 1970s. Leader Ervil LeBaron ordered his thirteen wives and various armed lieutenants to kill "false prophets" in other sects, as well as dissenters in his own ranks—even his own daughter and brother. Since LeBaron died in prison in 1982, more than a dozen of his disciples have been shot to death in sect rivalry. One of LeBaron's fifty-four children, Richard LeBaron, murdered a defector and his eight-year-old daughter in Houston in 1988. The son was sentenced to prison in 1993.

This tradition of religious madness continued spectacularly in a 1993 American trauma now known as Waco.

Waco and the Branch Davidians

(AP/Wide World Photos)

15

Waco and the Branch Davidians

Most of the world was transfixed in 1993 when a band of armed cultists died in a fiery showdown with government police at Waco, Texas. But few people knew that the Waco tragedy was part of a bizarre sequence that began 150 years earlier with a historic religious fiasco.

In the 1830s, a New England Baptist preacher, William Miller, computed from obscure prophecies in the Book of Daniel that Christ would return to Earth between March 21, 1843, and March 21, 1844. Miller began warning of the approaching apocalypse, in which the redeemed would find eternal joy and the wicked would meet destruction. By the 1840s, he had drawn to him nearly 100,000 followers.

When the fateful time arrived, the "Millerites" prayed and prayed and prayed, but nothing happened. Then William Miller reexamined the Bible verses and announced

211

that he had erred; the correct date would be October 22, 1844. As it neared, many of the faithful gave away their possessions, donned ornate garments, and waited on hilltops for the heavens to open. Again, a fizzle.

Many Millerites lost their faith, but a hardcore group held firm. Some of them insisted that doomsday actually had occurred on October 22, but it was a preparatory event in heaven that would be followed soon by Christ bursting forth onto Earth. This group formed the Seventh-day Adventist Church, a puritanical body that has been awaiting the Second Coming every day for the past 150 years.

As the Seventh-day Adventists grew to more than three million strong, some members felt that the church wasn't straitlaced enough. In the 1930s, a Los Angeles Adventist, Victor Houteff, declared that Christ wouldn't return until an ultra-pure church was ready to greet Him. So Houteff opened a Waco commune for pure Christians, calling them Davidian Seventh-day Adventists.

He died in 1955, and the Davidians prayerfully awaited his resurrection. When it didn't happen, his widow, Florence, took over. She proclaimed that Christ would return on Easter Day 1959. Hundreds of believers around the country quit their jobs, sold their belongings, and hurried to Waco for the rapture. Wrong again.

Once more, the disillusioned departed and a diehard group persisted. A member named Ben Roden took command and named the survivors Branch Davidians. He died in 1978, leaving the commune, called Mount Carmel, to his widow, Lois, and his son, George.

Soon afterward, a twenty-three-year-old Texas Adventist named Vernon Howell, a ninth-grade dropout, moved into the compound (and reportedly became the lover of the sixty-seven-year-old widow). He had hypnotic charisma, and he electrified the others with his inspired revelations of the coming apocalypse.

He married the fourteen-year-old daughter of a commune couple but soon declared that God had commanded him to establish a House of David, in which he was to have as many wives as King David. He bedded more than a dozen commune females—one barely eleven, another fifty. He gave each a Star of David to wear as an emblem that she had been chosen by the king.

After Lois Roden died in 1986, her son, George, vied with Howell for command. Roden won, temporarily. Howell was forced out of the commune at gunpoint. He and his followers wandered several months like nomads. Then in 1987, Howell's band returned to challenge Roden for leadership.

Roden proposed an epic contest: From a graveyard, he dug up the corpse of an eighty-five-year-old woman and declared that whoever could resurrect her would be the true prophet of Mount Carmel. Howell evaded, urging police to arrest Roden for corpse abuse.

Then Howell and seven armed supporters crept into Mount Carmel after midnight. Roden, armed with an Uzi machine gun, engaged the intruders in a firefight. He was wounded slightly in the hand and chest. Howell's band was charged with attempted murder, and released on bond.

Next, Roden was jailed for contempt of court because he filed grossly obscene motions in an unrelated case. While he was locked up, Howell moved his followers back into the compound and took over. His group's subsequent trial for attempted murder ended in acquittals. The dethroned Roden later killed a man and was sent to a state mental hospital.

Reigning as sole prophet, Howell preached that he was an angel sent by God to implement the Second Coming. He said God ordained him to move to Israel and convert the Jews, which would trigger the Battle of Armageddon and make Earth a paradise for the surviving faithful. Howell visited Israel but failed to convert the Jews.

Traveling around the globe, the dynamic young prophet attracted converts who sold their possessions, gave their money to him, and followed him to Waco to live in the compound. In 1989, he proclaimed that all women at Mount Carmel were his brides, and the rest of the men must remain celibate. Some married couples rebelled and left. Others, utterly dominated by him, obeyed.

Temporarily, Howell started a Branch Davidian group at La Verne, California, where he established a house for eighteen of his "wives." In 1990, Howell changed his name to David Koresh and began preaching that the great doomsday battle would occur in Texas. He and his lieutenants bought hundreds of guns, including semi-automatic weapons, plus ammunition, gas masks, grenades, and other war supplies. That's what precipitated the tragedy.

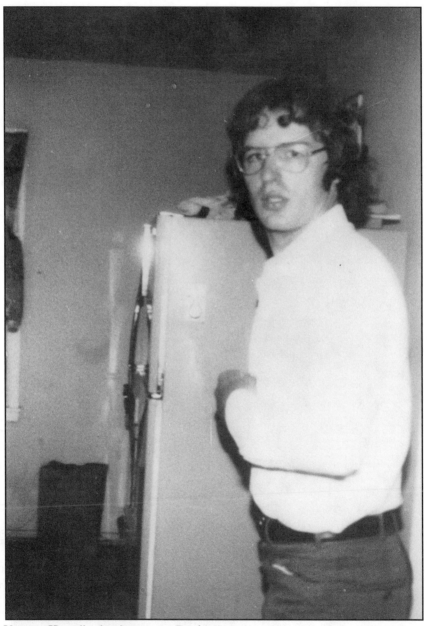

Vernon Howell, also known as David Koresh, cult leader of the Branch Davidians. (AP/Wide World Photos)

The Branch Davidian compound near Waco, Texas. (AP/Wide World Photos)

The Treasury Department's Bureau of Alcohol, Tobacco, and Firearms (BATF) heard reports of illegal guns in the Waco commune, and studied how to disarm the cult. Meanwhile, the State Department received alarms from Australians whose relatives were in the compound, and who feared that a mass suicide was imminent. Then a Waco newspaper threw a world spotlight on the situation in February 1993 by printing a front-page series on the odd sexual and theological happenings in Mount Carmel.

A special BATF swat team was brought in to serve search warrants and confiscate the guns. As the agents approached the cluster of buildings on February 28, war erupted. In the horrifying gunfight, four BATF agents and six cultists were killed. The federal police pulled back and a seven-week siege ensued.

During the long standoff, Koresh released twenty-two children and fourteen adults from the barricaded buildings. He promised to surrender if radio and television stations would broadcast a tape-recorded sermon by him. They did as he asked but Koresh never surrendered. He announced that he was awaiting "further instruction from God." Then he said he would surrender upon finishing a divinely inspired explanation of the Seven Seals, which are mentioned in the Book of Revelation.

FBI agents decided not to wait. On April 19, 1993, they used armored vehicles to punch holes in the besieged buildings and inject tear gas. Suddenly a fire flared, swiftly engulfing the whole compound. Koresh and 78 followers died, including 18 children. Later examinations found that Koresh and several others had been shot.

The FBI and BATF were widely criticized for using assault tactics at Waco. Gun groups argued that the cultists simply had defended themselves. Eleven surviving cultists were charged with murder for their part in the February 28 battle. But when they came to trial in 1994, they were ruled innocent of murder. Five of the eleven were convicted of manslaughter, for which they drew sentences of forty years each. Three of the remaining six were convicted of lesser offenses and received sentences ranging from five to twenty years.

In the aftermath of Waco, scholars mulled over the meaning of the tragedy. Theologian John Roth of Claremont-McKenna College in California ruefully acknowledged:

> Religion is as full of pathology as it is of health and life-giving resources. . . . Outbreaks like these only confirm people's deepest suspicions about religion: that it's manipulative, exploitive of the naïve, and a bad deal. . . .
>
> The idea of having to fight to protect what you believe is an ancient dimension of religious life. Even today, in places like Serbia and India, people are quite prepared to take up the sword or a gun to protect what they hold sacred.
>
> We're approaching the end of the millennium, and it wouldn't be surprising to see more instances of armed believers anticipating the end of the world.*

---

*Newhouse News Service, 1993.

A woman calling herself "a Talmidad" walks with her dogs near the Branch Davidian compound as she carries her cross on a mission across the country. (AP/Wide World Photos)

16

A Decade of Furious Faith

Personally, I think humanity has a streak of madness, a precinct of the mind where magic expels reason. Without a shred of evidence, all societies have invented invisible heavens, hells, gods, devils, angels, demons, and the like. "Man cannot make a worm, yet he will make gods by the dozen," Montaigne wrote in 1580. Or, as the Bible says in II Kings: "Every nation made gods of their own."

Anthropologist Desmond Morris said religions spring from three urges: "man's need to protect himself from the threat of death; man's need for a super-parent; and man's need for a super-leader. A god that offers an afterlife in another world, that protects his 'children' regardless of their age, and that offers them devotion to a grand cause and a socially unifying purpose, triggers off a powerful reaction in the human animal."* Morris said that priests perpetuate their power and privileges by posing as agents of the unseen gods, leading elaborate rituals to them, fanning devotion to them, and fomenting suspicion of rival faiths. They seek to punish anyone who doubts the mystical deities.

Believing in spirit realms might be harmless, like believing in fairies or werewolves, were it not for the potential for horror. Religious killing occurs in several forms. In previous centuries, it included human sacrifice, the burning of "witches," and holy wars to spread the faith. In the 1990s, it includes executing "blasphemers" who defame the holies and "infidels" who hold different beliefs (such as the Baha'is among Shi'ites in Iran).

An odd religious horror killed a teen-age Muslim girl in 1994 at Roubaix, France, not far from the Belgian border. Relatives said Louisa Lardjoune was possessed by the devil, so the *imam* of the local mosque led an exorcism. The girl was beaten, strangled, and a gallon of salt water was forced down her throat. After she died, the *imam* told police: "The devil hates salt water. It's the devil that killed Louisa." He and the mosque president were charged with "torture and acts of barbary causing death."

But the worst death toll arises from ethnic factors. Each faith imprints a special identity on believers, isolating them from those who worship differently. The cultural gulf can breed suspicion, hostility, political ferment, riots, terrorism, and open warfare.

Manwatching, p. 152.

As a newspaper editor, I see hundreds of daily news reports, and the number of religious cruelties among them is astounding. Newspapers deal with real-life situations, and one such reality is that religion causes people to commit horrendous acts every day, somewhere around the globe.

For example, Pentecostal evangelists are converting some of Mexico's Catholics to the Protestant "talking-in-tongues" faith. This sometimes causes clashes between Catholic and Pentecostal crowds. The March 19, 1990, issue of *Christianity Today* reported the following:

> Hostilities between Mexico's Catholics and Protestants reached a new high last month when an interdenominational prayer meeting attended by some 160 evangelicals in the Mexico City area was violently broken up by a mob of several thousand Catholics armed with stones, machetes, and sticks. Virtually all of those attending the meeting were injured. . . . Witnesses said that an all-night prayer meeting being held on the slopes of the Ajusco volcano in the southeast section of Mexico City had been in progress for several hours when crowds yelling "Kill them!" and "This is a Catholic town!" converged on the group. . . .
>
> In 1989 alone, attacks against evangelicals took the lives of at least five believers, injured dozens more, caused hundreds to flee homelands, and destroyed or closed countless churches. . . . More than thirty churches in the state of Hidalgo are closed and unable to function due to threats of violence against those congregations.

Nearly all the mayhem is wrought by simpleminded believers categorized as fundamentalists. Literally, fundamentalism means belief in the word-for-word truth of sacred scriptures, entailing *real* heavens, *real* hells, *real* miracles, *real* devils, *real* houri nymphs, and so forth. Fundamentalists of all faiths usually are puritanical individuals who strive to suppress sex, punish nonconformists, and stigmatize holders of other beliefs.

As education rose in Western democracies, fundamentalism faded from several mainline Protestant denominations. Their supernaturalism grew blurry, they tolerated other doctrines, and they became a counterpoint to conservative excesses. Religion of this "liberal" sort doesn't cause bloodshed.

But a strange phenomenon occurred: The liberal churches are dying. In Europe their attendance has shrunk to a tiny remnant. In the United States, Presbyterians have lost 25 percent of their members since the 1960s; Episcopalians, 28 percent; Methodists, 18 percent; the United Church of Christ, 20 percent; and the Disciples of Christ, 43 percent. Collectively, they've dropped five million members while the U.S. population grew by fifty million.

Evidently, educated people are losing their need for religion. However, fundamentalism, the domain of the less-educated, has boomed in the United States and in much of the world. As the ranks of fundamentalists swell, conflicts worsen, especially in poverty zones, where believers clash with rival sects or strive to replace secular governments with theocracies.

Pundits, authors, journalists and other observers have noted the upsurge in fundamentalist violence since the end of the Cold War:

Early in 1990, as the Soviet Union was crumbling, H. D. S. Greenway of the *Boston Globe* speculated prophetically that "the breakup of the Soviet Empire will be plagued by the same four apocalyptical horsemen that ran roughshod over the world following the breakup of the British, French, and Ottoman empires: ethnic hatred, religious intolerance, communal violence, and shortsighted nationalism. For all its faults, the dead hand of colonialism did keep historical rivalries in check." Already, he wrote, Alexandria, once the cosmopolitan jewel of Egypt, had become "a hard Islamic fundamentalist town." With uncanny accuracy, Greenway predicted: "There is a strong possibility that Yugoslavia itself will disintegrate in the coming decade." He added that sectarian warfare is "the triumph of hate over self-interest."

*   *   *

At the end of the year, the *Christian Century's* December issue said that the top religion story of 1990 was that, after the fall of the Berlin Wall, "the world seemed more than ever divided by religious parties and by ethnic and nationalist sentiments intimately tied to religious beliefs."

*   *   *

Scholar George Weigel declared: "The unsecularization of the world is one of the dominant social facts of life in the late twentieth century."

*   *   *

Nobel Prize winner Elie Wiesel, writing in *Parade* magazine in 1992, deplored the rising fanaticism that "turns religion into a personal battlefield that is dangerous to others and demeaning to the very faith it professes to cherish." He quoted Nietzsche: "Madness is the result not of uncertainty but certainty."

*   *   *

French savant Gilles Kepel published *The Revenge of God*, a study of rising fundamentalism among Catholics, Protestants, Jews, and Muslims. "These religious movements are now voicing the claims of many people who have not found their place in the sun," he said in a 1994 interview. According to Kepel, fanatics "go back to the sacred texts" and choose commandments that fit their radicalism. "The assassins of Sadat in 1981 did this," he said. "So did the Jewish underground in Israel that plotted to blow up the al-Aqsa mosque."

*   *   *

"Fundamentalism is growing because of the failure of other 'isms'—Baathism [secular politics of Iraq], socialism, communism," commented former Middle East diplomat Richard Murphy in *Newsweek*.

*   *   *

Harvard professor Samuel Huntington wrote in 1993 that since the ideological contest between superpowers ceased, the world has shifted to a new era in which "the dominating source of conflict will be cultural. . . . The fault lines between civilizations will be the battle lines of the future." He said civilizations derive from "history, language, culture, tradition, and, most importantly, religion." Faith is surging in many poorer lands, he said, as seen in "the Hinduization of India" and "the re-Islamization of the Middle East." Writing in *Foreign Affairs*, he said: "As the ideological division of Europe has disappeared, the cultural division of Europe between Western Christianity and Orthodox Christianity and Islam has reemerged. . . . On the northern border of Islam, conflict has increasingly erupted between Orthodox and Muslim peoples, including the carnage in Bosnia."

*   *   *

Commenting on the breakup of Yugoslavia, columnist Anthony Lewis said in the *New York Times* that 1993 "left at least one mark on modern history. In that year the principle of the ethno-religious state was established in Europe."

* * *

Presbyterian minister Robert Meneilly wrote in the
March-April 1994 issue of *Liberty* magazine that fanatic
faith is the "greatest health hazard," a worse danger than
"the old threat of communism." He said: "Look at the
hot-spots of the earth today: religious extremists are
lighting fuses in Northern Ireland, Israel, Bosnia, and the
United States, and fomenting all kinds of 'culture wars.'
Religion can breed harassment, bigotry, prejudice, intolerance, and deception. . . . We Christians must admit that
our religion has propagated, in the name of Jesus, devilish
acts, bloody wars, awful persecutions, hate crimes, and
political chaos."

* * *

U.S. District Judge John L. Kane said in a Denver speech
in June 1987: "Religious oppression is older than the pyramids of Egypt and as current as the butchering of members
of the Baha'i faith in Iran today. One of the dominant
themes of human history, religious intolerance, unhappily
continues with the ferocity and relentlessness of all that
is evil in the human spirit."

* * *

United Nations Secretary General Boutros Boutros-Ghali
warned in November 1993 that "ethnic conflict poses as great
a danger to common world security as did the Cold War."

*　　*　　*

Lance Morrow of *Time* wrote in March of 1993 that the 1990s have been afflicted by "irrational religious tribalisms." He said: "If you scratch any aggressive tribalism, or nationalism, you usually find beneath its surface a religious core, some older binding energy of belief or superstition. . . . Faith, the sweetest refuge and consolation, may harden, by perverse miracle, into a sword—or anyway into a club or a torch or an assault rifle. Religious hatreds tend to be merciless and absolute."

*　　*　　*

Vice President Albert Gore, speaking at a Religious Freedom Day ceremony at Richmond, Virginia, on January 14, 1994, noted: "Even as we celebrate our religious liberty today, killing in the name of religion goes on all around the world. At this moment, the Muslims of Sarajevo are being shelled by artillery from the supposedly Christian Serbs in the mountains above the helpless city. The peaceful, inoffensive adherents of the Baha'i faith in Iran are imprisoned and murdered by the Iranian government. Their crime? The Baha'is believe in the spiritual unity of humankind. Saddam Hussein carries on a campaign of terror against the Shi'ite Muslims in his Iraq. Muslim fundamentalists in Egypt machine gun tourists. Hindus and Muslims in the Indian subcontinent are at each other's throats. Northern Ireland blazes with gunfire between opposing sides who claim to worship the same Christ, as we pray for the success of the new initiative to bring them peace. Throughout history, religious wars have always been the most brutal and cruel and merciless."

All this is a grievous reality of the 1990s. Religion, despite its universal message of compassion, can mix with politics, poverty, tribalism, and social ferment to produce the destructive opposite of compassion. If the 1980s were the decade of dying communism, the 1990s may well be called the decade of furious faith.

Not even the gentle Buddhists of Tibet are immune. The Tibetans, who follow the Dalai Lama, believe that when a spiritual leader dies, his soul later is reincarnated in a newborn baby, who is destined to become the next leader. Since the new guru cannot be identified until he is old enough to show signs of divinity, each of Tibet's four Buddhist sects remains leaderless for years after an old guru's death. The Kargyud sect lost its leader in 1982, and spent a decade waiting for a holy child to become known. In March of 1994, the Associated Press reported that exiled monks in India proclaimed they had found the new living god, a ten-year-old boy. They staged a ceremony to present him. However, the ritual was mobbed by rival monks who believe that an eight-year-old boy living in Tibet is the true reincarnation. A riot ensued. Windows were smashed and buildings battered. The rivals finally were driven off by a barrage of rocks thrown by monks on rooftops.

Other Buddhist monks in Thailand have become big-money operators like America's TV evangelists, and, like their American counterparts, they are falling into scandals. Popular monk Phra Kittiwuttho was arrested in 1994 on charges of fraud in a $275,000 land sale. And "superstar" monk Yantra Ammarobhikku, who made a fortune by selling books and cassettes, was accused of sex flings that violated his celibacy oath.

A grotesque religious evil flared in 1994 in the Lebowa district of South Africa. The Associated Press reported in June of 1994 that repeatedly, after villagers died, shamans pointed to "witches" who supposedly caused the deaths, whereupon villagers set upon the accused and burned them alive in their homes. Sixty-five were executed in the first half of the year. Some entire families were doused with gasoline and immolated. Police said Lebowans traditionally have feared witches, but burnings didn't become common until recently.

As for the many types of religious killing, throughout history and in current headlines, a tragic irony is that all the horror rests on fantasy. Phoenicians sacrificed their children to Astarte, Adonis, and Moloch, yet these gods didn't exist. The parents killed their children for nothing. Similarly, Aztecs ripped out hearts for their feathered-serpent god, and Thugs strangled victims for Kali—all for figments of the imagination. Is current bloodshed over Lord Rama's 900,000-year-old birthplace and a whisker from Muhammad's beard any different?

Most of today's killing in the name of religion is laced with ethnic and cultural factors, yet at bottom is the faith that brands adherents with an indelible label and makes them enemies to people wearing a different label.

The irrational precinct of the mind which needs invisible spirits can be dangerous, and has brought untold misery. Thinking people must strive constantly to hold it in check.

Ironically, nations with fervent religion often have the worst social evils. For example, the United States has more churchgoing than any other major democracy, and it reports much higher rates of murder, rape, robbery, shootings, stabbings, drug use, unwed pregnancy, and the like, as well as occasional tragedies such as those at Waco and Jonestown, Guyana. There may be no link between the two conditions, but the saturation of religion has failed to prevent the severe crime level. As the chapters of this book have shown, societies rife with fundamentalism and religious tribalism are prone to sectarian violence. In contrast, England, Scandinavia, Canada, Japan, and such lands have scant churchgoing, yet their people are more inclined to live peaceably in accord with the social contract.

The evidence seems clear: To find living conditions that are safe, decent, orderly, and "civilized," avoid places with intense religion.

Epilogue

These additional religious horrors occurred late in 1994:

Two Louisiana sisters, Doretha Crawford and Beverly Johnson, were convicted in September 1994 of gouging out a third sister's eyes because they thought she was possessed by the devil. Fearing that Satan was pursuing them, the three sisters fled the town of Arcadia and wound up in Dallas, Texas, where they prayed loudly on a street for seven hours before the woman was blinded.

*   *   *

Flamboyant Arkansas evangelist Tony Alamo, known for raging tirades against the Catholic Church, was sentenced to six years in prison in September 1994 for tax evasion. At his trial, federal agents said the minister, fifty-nine, recently married himself to eight of his followers, two of them fifteen years old.

*   *   *

In October, in rural Switzerland near Geneva, about fifty members of a sect called the Cross and the Rose died in an apparent mass suicide. Police said most of the believers evidently suffocated themselves by securing plastic bags over their heads. The bodies of several children were found lying together. One member had been shot in the head. The tragedy was discovered by officers rushing to fight fires set in several buildings of the sect's farm northeast of Geneva, and three ski chalets southeast of Geneva.

A few hours earlier, in Quebec, Canada, a fire killed two people in the headquarters of a cult that had been stockpiling weapons to prepare for the end of the world. The group's leader was believed to be in Switzerland.

Select Bibliography

Abrahamian, Ervand. *Khomeinism: Essays on the Islamic Republic.* Berkeley: University of California Press, 1993.

Berry, Jason. *Lead Us Not Into Temptation: Catholic Priests and the Sexual Abuse of Children.* New York: Doubleday, 1992.

Blanchard, Dallas, and Terry Prewitt. *Religious Violence and Abortion: The Gideon Project.* Gainesville: University Press of Florida, 1993.

Bodansky, Yossef. *Target America: Terrorism in the U.S. Today.* New York: S.P.I. Books, 1993.

Earley, Pete. *Prophet of Death: The Mormon Blood-Atonement Killings.* New York: William Morrow & Co., 1991.

Elon, Amos. *Jerusalem: City of Mirrors.* Boston: Little, Brown & Co., 1989.

Filipovic, Zlata. *Zlata's Diary: A Child's Life in Sarajevo.* New York: Viking Penguin, 1994.

Fortune, Marie M. *Is Nothing Sacred?: When Sex Invades the Pastoral Relationship.* San Francisco: Harper, 1989.

Gaylor, Annie Laurie. *Betrayal of Trust: Clergy Abuse of Children*. Madison, Wis.: Freedom from Religion Foundation, 1988.

Hunter, F. Robert. *The Palestinian Uprising: A War by Other Means*. Berkeley: University of California Press, 1993.

Kaplan, Robert D. *Balkan Ghosts: A Journey Through History*. St. Martin's Press, 1993.

Keegan, John. *Waffen SS: The Asphalt Soldiers*. New York: Ballantine Books, 1970.

Kepel, Gilles. *Muslim Extremism in Egypt: The Prophet and the Pharaoh*. Berkeley: University of California Press, 1986.

———. *The Revenge of God: The Resurgence of Islam, Christianity, and Judaism in the Modern World*. University Park, Penn.: Penn State Press, 1994.

Laaser, Mark R. *The Secret Sin: Healing the Wounds of Sexual Addiction*. Grand Rapids, Mich.: Zondervan, 1992.

Marty, Martin E., and R. Scott Appleby. *The Glory and the Power: The Fundamentalist Challenge to the Modern World*. Boston: Beacon Press, 1992.

Mojzes, Paul. *Yugoslavia Inferno: Ethnoreligious Warfare in the Balkans*. New York: Continuum, 1994.

Morris, Desmond. *Manwatching: A Field Guide to Human Behavior*. Bergenfield, N.J.: Harry N. Abrams, Inc., 1977.

O'Brien, Conor Cruise. *God Land: Reflections on Religion and Nationalism*. Cambridge, Mass.: Harvard University Press, 1988.

O'Leary, Stephen D. *Arguing the Apocalypse: A Theory of Millennial Rhetoric*. New York: Oxford University Press, 1993.

Riesbrodt, Martin. *Pious Passion: The Emergence of Modern Fundamentalism in the United States and Iran.* Berkeley: University of California Press, 1993.

Rossetti, Stephen J. *Slayer of the Soul: Child Sexual Abuse and the Catholic Church.* Mystic, Conn.: 23rd Publications, 1990.

West, Rebecca. *Black Lamb and Grey Falcon: A Journey Through Yugoslavia.* New York: The Viking Press, 1941.

Wright, Robin. *Sacred Rage: The Wrath of Militant Islam.* New York: Linden Press/Simon & Schuster, 1985.